THE BEST OF MARTHA STEWART LIVING

Desserts

Our Favorite Recipes
for Every Season
and Every Occasion

Clarkson Potter/Publishers

New York

Thanks to the many food editors, stylists, art directors, photographers, and editors whose inspirational ideas and recipes make up this volume. Thanks also to the entire staff of Martha Stewart Living Omnimedia and to everyone at Oxmoor House, Clarkson Potter, Satellite Graphics, and Quebecor Printing whose work and dedication helped produce this book.

Originally published in book form by Martha Stewart Living Omnimedia LLC in 1998. Published simultaneously by Clarkson N. Potter, Inc., Oxmoor House, Inc., and Leisure Arts.

Most of the recipes and photographs in this work were previously published in MARTHA STEWART LIVING.

Published by Clarkson N. Potter, Inc., 201 East 50th Street, New York, NY 10022. Member of the Crown Publishing Group. Random House, Inc. New York, Toronto, London, Sydney, Auckland www.randomhouse.com Clarkson N. Potter, Potter, and colophon are trademarks of Clarkson N. Potter, Inc.

Printed in the United States of America.

Library of Congress Cataloging-in-Publication Data is available upon request.

ISBN 0-609-80339-5

10 9 8 7 6 5 4 3 2 1 First Edition

Senior Editor: Bruce Shostak Art Director: Linda Kocur Writer: Trish Hall Copy Editor: Kyle T. Blood Design Production Associate: Curtis Smith

Desserts

DATE			

Contents

Introduction

I have always loved desserts, and I always will. A beautiful tart with a piquant and tasty filling can end almost any dinner in the most satisfactory fashion. Little lemon soufflés, perfectly made with high crowns and tender centers, will most certainly elicit the oohs and aahs that every host desires. A towering cake, light and moist, with exacting texture and crumb, can be served plain, filled, or enhanced with a delectable sauce; it will garner appreciation and be the glory of any party. * This book is filled with desserts that are either modest or fancy, embellished or unadorned. The recipes, which have been carefully tested, should ensure success—many are easy enough that even the uninitiated cook or baker can experience excellent results and savor delicious flavors. For so many of us today, appetizers, salads, and especially main courses are often made with much attention to healthy ingredients and a concern for healthy living. But desserts, to be the most wonderful, should never withhold those ingredients that result in the best taste, form, and texture. Fresh butter, heavy cream, farm-fresh eggs, and best-quality flour are basic to sweet-making. The cardinal rule in making desserts should always be "Do not skimp!" I share this credo with the finest pastry chefs and cooks everywhere. When a recipe calls for lemon juice, we agree that the juice should be freshly squeezed and used immediately, so that none of the flavor is lost or compromised. Apples for tarts or pies or sauce must be flavorful and well-suited for the job: sugary and firm for a galette, juicy and sour for pies, red-skinned and white-fleshed for applesauce. For chocolate desserts, use only the finest chocolate, and never abuse its delicate quality: Melt it gently, mix it with other ingredients cautiously, and be careful never to overheat it or burn it. * I and the food editors of Martha Stewart Living try hard to create classic recipes with a twist, recipes that we hope will live a long time. My wish is that they will become as much a part of your repertoire as they have become an important part of ours.

Martha Stewart

1 *This lovely lemon cake offers layers of luxurious textures and tastes, with both sweetened whipped cream and custardy lemon curd. Although this cake would be wonderful any time of the year, it's best when the berries piled high on top are picked by hand or bought fresh.*

chapter one

Cakes

Each one is a delicious
triumph of taste and technique —
and surprisingly easy to make

Cakes are so central to birthdays, weddings, and other red-letter days that it's easy to forget that they are also an everyday food. The freshly baked cake waiting on the kitchen counter is very much a part of the life of a home. Children will sneak by six or seven times a day, scooping up crumbs and any extra icing, while adults persist in their curious habit of scheduling a slice after dinner. * The cakes in this chapter range from a single layer to a towering construction filled with fruit and whipped cream. Each has its time to shine. Complex cakes with multiple flavors, like our ginger-pecan cake with crème-fraîche filling and caramel frosting, are clearly for special occasions, perhaps a promotion at the office. The satisfyingly dense applesauce cake is perfect for an unhurried weekend breakfast. Even a relaxed summer dinner of salad and hamburgers on the patio is elevated by the arrival of a chocolate cake. * If you haven't done a lot of baking, you will be more comfortable starting with a simple cake, like the cranberry upside-down cake or the pecan torte with apricot filling. Don't underestimate their power to dazzle; both are beautiful on a pretty plate or cake stand. * Whether you're a beginner or an experienced baker, keep in mind a few basic rules: Always bring all the ingredients to room temperature before using them. Always follow the recipe to the letter because baking is a precise science—if you decide to experiment, your efforts may yield a pancake. Always use parchment paper, when called for, to keep cakes from sticking to pans. And don't take anything for granted. If a recipe calls for a two-inch-deep pan, measure yours—don't just eyeball it. * A homemade cake will always be imbued with rich feelings that separate it from anything bought from a bakery, so take a moment to remember why you're baking. If you create traditions with cakes, you will be shaping delicious memories that will last a lifetime.

1 1-2-3-4 lemon cake

1 cup (2 sticks) unsalted butter,
　room temperature, plus more
　for pans
3 cups sifted all-purpose flour,
　plus more for pans
1 tablespoon baking powder
1 teaspoon baking soda
½ teaspoon salt
2 cups granulated sugar
4 large eggs, lightly beaten
1¼ cups buttermilk
1½ teaspoons pure vanilla extract
　Grated zest of 2 lemons
　Lemon Curd (recipe follows)
　Sweetened Whipped Cream
　(recipe follows)
12 ounces assorted fresh berries
　Confectioners' sugar,
　for dusting

The name of this old-fashioned cake comes from the simple formula used for measuring the main ingredients: one cup butter, two cups sugar, three cups flour, and four eggs. | **makes one 8-inch-round layer cake**

1. Heat oven to 350°; arrange two racks in center of oven. Butter two 8-by-2-inch round cake pans; line bottoms with parchment paper. Dust bottoms and sides of pans with flour; tap out any excess.

2. In a large bowl, sift together the flour, baking powder, baking soda, and salt.

3. In the bowl of an electric mixer fitted with paddle attachment, cream butter on medium speed until softened, 1 to 2 minutes. Gradually add granulated sugar, beating on medium speed until lightened, 3 to 4 minutes; scrape down sides once or twice. Drizzle in the eggs, a little at a time, beating after each addition until the batter is no longer slick, about 5 minutes; stop once or twice to scrape down sides.

4. On low speed, alternately add the flour mixture and buttermilk, a little of each at a time, beginning and ending with the flour mixture. Beat in the vanilla and the lemon zest.

5. Divide the batter evenly between the prepared pans. Bake 25 minutes, then rotate the pans in the oven for even browning. Continue baking until a cake tester inserted into the center of each cake comes out clean, 10 to 20 minutes more. Transfer pans to wire racks to cool, 15 minutes. Turn out cakes; set on racks, tops up, until completely cool.

6. Remove the parchment from bottom of each cake. Using a serrated knife, slice each layer in half horizontally. Set aside the prettiest domed layer for the top of cake. Place another domed layer, dome-side down, on a serving platter. Spread 1 cup lemon curd over surface to within ½ inch from edges. Place the second cake layer over the first, and spread another 1 cup curd over top. Repeat with third cake layer and remaining cup curd. Transfer partially assembled cake to the refrigerator.

7. Just before serving, place reserved dome on top of cake. Spoon sweetened whipped cream over the top. Sprinkle with mixed berries, and dust with confectioners' sugar through a fine sieve.

lemon curd | **makes about 3 cups**

This recipe makes a nice thick curd that you can use to fill any layer cake.

12 large egg yolks
　Grated zest of 2 lemons plus 1
　cup freshly squeezed lemon
　juice (about 6 lemons)
1½ cups sugar
1 cup (2 sticks) unsalted butter,
　chilled and cut into pieces

1. Pass the egg yolks through a strainer set over a heavy saucepan to remove any traces of white. Add the lemon zest, lemon juice, and sugar. Whisk to combine. Set over medium heat; stir constantly with a wooden spoon, making sure to stir all the sides and edges of the saucepan. Cook until mixture is thick enough to coat the back of the wooden spoon, 20 to 25 minutes.

2. Remove saucepan from heat. Add the butter, one piece at a time, stirring with the wooden spoon into a smooth mixture. Transfer curd to a medium bowl. Lay plastic wrap directly on the surface to prevent a skin from forming, and chill until firm, at least 1 hour.

sweetened whipped cream | **makes 1⅓ cups**

Prepare this whipped cream just before serving the cake.

⅔ cup heavy cream
½ teaspoon pure vanilla extract
2 tablespoons confectioners' sugar

Whip the heavy cream in the bowl of an electric mixer fitted with the whisk attachment on medium speed until soft peaks form, 2 to 4 minutes. Add the vanilla and confectioners' sugar; continue whipping on medium speed until the soft peaks return, 2 to 3 minutes. Use immediately.

2 *A slice of this classic cake, which almost requires a glass of milk at its side, will end every chocolate lover's quest. Dutch-process cocoa provides the rich color and strong flavor; the frosting is made from semisweet chocolate morsels and whipping cream. If you plan to serve the cake for an afternoon party, be sure to start it in the morning: The frosting needs about two hours to chill before it will become spreadable.*

2 moist devil's food cake

1½ cups (3 sticks) unsalted butter,
   plus more for pans
¾ cup Dutch-process cocoa
   powder, plus more for pans
2¼ cups sugar
1 tablespoon pure vanilla extract
4 large eggs, lightly beaten
3 cups sifted cake flour
   (not self-rising)
1 teaspoon baking soda
½ teaspoon salt
1 cup milk
   Mrs. Milman's Chocolate
   Frosting (recipe follows)

Great swoops of glossy frosting make this a wonderfully exuberant cake with a dark backdrop for birthday candles. But this cake is just as suitable for afternoon snacks or a Sunday supper. It keeps well for several days stored on the counter: Cover with plastic wrap or a glass dome to keep frosting from drying out. | **makes one 8-inch-round layer cake**

1. Heat oven to 350°; arrange two racks in center of oven. Butter three 8-by-2-inch round cake pans; line bottoms with parchment. Dust bottoms and sides of pans with cocoa powder; tap out any excess. Sift cocoa into a medium bowl, and whisk in ½ cup boiling water. Set aside to cool.

2. In the bowl of an electric mixer fitted with the paddle attachment, cream the butter on low speed until light and fluffy. Gradually beat in the sugar until light and fluffy, 3 to 4 minutes, scraping down sides twice. Beat in the vanilla. Drizzle in the eggs, a little at a time, beating between each addition until the batter is no longer slick, scraping down the sides twice.

3. In a large bowl, sift together the flour, baking soda, and salt. Whisk the milk into reserved cocoa mixture. With mixer on low speed, alternately add the flour and cocoa mixtures to the batter, a little of each at a time, starting and ending with the flour mixture.

4. Divide batter evenly among the three prepared pans. Bake until a cake tester inserted into center of each layer comes out clean, 35 to 45 minutes, rotating the pans for even baking. Transfer layers to wire racks; let cool, 15 minutes. Turn out cakes, and return to racks, tops up, until completely cool.

5. Remove parchment from bottoms of cakes. Reserve the prettiest layer for the top. Place one cake layer on a serving platter; spread 1½ cups chocolate frosting over the top. Add the second cake layer, and spread with another 1½ cups frosting. Top with third cake layer. Cover outside of cake with the remaining 3 cups frosting. Serve.

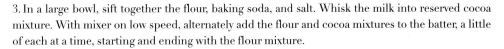

mrs. milman's chocolate frosting | **makes 6 cups**

24 ounces Nestlé semisweet
   chocolate morsels
4 cups whipping cream
1 teaspoon light corn syrup

While this frosting is cooling, you'll need to stir it as instructed; otherwise, the frosting around the edge of the bowl will harden and the frosting at the center will remain liquid. The finished frosting should have a consistent texture. Lois Milman, the creator of the frosting, always uses Nestlé morsels and makes only one batch at a time. Spread the icing as soon as it is sufficiently chilled; it holds its shape well on the cake.

1. Place the chocolate morsels and cream in a heavy saucepan. Cook over low heat, stirring constantly with a rubber spatula, until combined and thickened, between 20 and 25 minutes. Increase the heat to medium low; cook, stirring, 3 minutes more. Remove pan from heat.

2. Stir in the corn syrup. Transfer frosting to a large metal bowl. Chill until cool enough to spread, about 2 hours, checking and stirring every 15 to 20 minutes. Use immediately.

3 coconut cake

¾ cup (1½ sticks) unsalted butter, room temperature, plus more for pans

2 cups sifted cake flour (not self-rising), plus more for pans

½ teaspoon baking powder

½ teaspoon baking soda

¼ teaspoon salt

1 cup superfine sugar

4 large egg yolks, lightly beaten

⅔ cup sour cream

1 teaspoon pure vanilla extract

11 ounces (about 3¾ cups) sweetened angel-flake coconut
Coconut-Cream Filling (recipe follows)
Seven-Minute Frosting (recipe follows)

If this cake doesn't disappear instantly, keep it in the refrigerator. | **makes one 6-inch-round layer cake**

1. Heat oven to 350°; arrange two racks in center of oven. Butter three 6-by-2-inch round cake pans; line each with a circle of parchment paper. Dust the bottoms and the sides of the pans with flour; tap out any excess. Set the prepared pans aside.

2. In a large bowl, sift together the flour, baking powder, baking soda, and salt.

3. In the bowl of an electric mixer fitted with the paddle attachment, cream butter on medium-low speed until fluffy, 1 to 2 minutes. Gradually add sugar; keep beating until mixture is fluffy and light in color, about 3 minutes. Drizzle in egg yolks a little at a time, beating on medium-low speed between each addition until batter is no longer slick. Beat until fluffy again, about 3 minutes more.

4. Alternately add the flour mixture and the sour cream to the batter, a little of each at a time, starting and ending with the flour mixture. Beat in the vanilla.

5. Divide batter among prepared cake pans. Bake until a cake tester inserted into center of each cake comes out clean, 30 to 40 minutes, rotating pans in the oven, if needed, for even browning. Transfer pans to wire racks to cool, 15 minutes. Turn out cakes; let cool completely on racks, tops up.

6. Remove parchment from cakes. Using a serrated knife, slice each layer in half horizontally. Set aside prettiest domed layer for top. Place another domed layer, dome-side down, on a serving platter. Sprinkle 2 to 3 tablespoons flaked coconut over surface. Spread a generous ½ cup coconut-cream filling over the coconut flakes. Add another cake layer, and repeat sprinkling and spreading process. Continue making layers, finishing with reserved dome. Chill until firm, about 1 hour.

7. Frost the outside of the cake with seven-minute frosting. Sprinkle remaining coconut flakes all over cake while frosting remains soft. Store at room temperature.

coconut-cream filling | makes 4 cups

6 large egg yolks

¾ cup sugar

6 tablespoons cornstarch

⅛ teaspoon salt

3 cups milk

4 ounces (1½ cups) sweetened angel-flake coconut

1½ teaspoons pure vanilla extract

1 teaspoon unsalted butter

This filling may be made up to one day ahead and kept, tightly covered, in the refrigerator.

1. Place egg yolks in a large bowl; whisk to combine; set bowl aside.

2. Combine sugar, cornstarch, and salt in a saucepan. Gradually whisk in milk. Cook, stirring, over medium heat until mixture thickens and comes to a boil, 10 to 12 minutes. Remove from heat.

3. Whisk ½ cup hot milk mixture into the reserved egg yolks to temper. Slowly pour warm yolks into the saucepan, stirring constantly. Cook slowly, stirring over medium-low heat until mixture begins to bubble, 5 to 6 minutes. Remove from heat. Stir in coconut and vanilla.

4. Transfer filling to a medium mixing bowl. Lightly butter a piece of plastic wrap, and lay it directly on top of filling to prevent a skin from forming. Chill until firm, at least 1 hour.

seven-minute frosting | makes 3 cups

2 large egg whites

1½ cups sugar

2 teaspoons light corn syrup

¼ teaspoon cream of tartar

½ teaspoon pure vanilla extract

1. Combine the egg whites, sugar, corn syrup, cream of tartar, and 5 tablespoons cold water in a heat-proof bowl; hold the bowl over a pan of rapidly boiling water.

2. Using a handheld electric mixer, beat mixture on medium-low speed 4 minutes. Beat 3 minutes more on high, or until soft peaks form. Remove from heat; add the vanilla. Continue beating until glossy and spreadable, 3 to 5 minutes more. Use frosting immediately.

3 Each bite of this sky-high creation is a different experience, depending on what combination of sour-cream cake, coconut-cream filling, and seven-minute frosting makes it onto the fork. The recipe makes a teetering six-layer cake, but if you prefer the look of a five-layer cake, save the extra layer for a delicious midnight snack.

4 *Lemon-meringue cake is inspired by the classic pie. Layers of lemon-chiffon cake and lemon curd are encased in a swirling cloud of meringue that is browned very briefly just before serving. When beating egg whites for the meringue, be sure to start with clean, dry equipment. Don't over-beat the whites; they should hold their shape but should not be dry.*

5 *These little cakes are filled with lumps of ganache that turn to molten chocolate in the oven. Because most of the preparation is done ahead of time—the cakes go directly from the freezer into the oven, requiring no last-minute work—they are perfect for a romantic dinner for two or a small party. Here they are dusted with confectioners' sugar and served on early-nineteenth-century Choisy dessert plates.*

4 lemon-meringue cake

1 cup plus 2 tablespoons sifted
 cake flour (not self-rising)
1½ teaspoons baking powder
¼ teaspoon salt
3 large eggs, separated,
 room temperature
¾ cup superfine sugar
¼ cup vegetable oil
1 teaspoon grated orange zest
 plus 4 tablespoons freshly
 squeezed orange juice
1 teaspoon grated lemon zest plus
 2 tablespoons freshly squeezed
 lemon juice
 Pinch cream of tartar
 Lemon-Curd Filling
 (recipe follows)
 Swiss Meringue (recipe follows)
 Vegetable oil, for baking sheet

This small cake is baked in a seven-inch tube pan. If you want to make a larger cake, double the recipe, use a ten-inch tube pan, and increase the baking time to sixty minutes. When slicing this cake, run a knife under hot water, then wipe dry, and cut. Repeat as you slice more servings. | **makes one 7-inch-round cake**

1. Heat oven to 325°. In a large bowl, sift together the flour, baking powder, and salt twice. Set aside.

2. Place the egg yolks in the large bowl of an electric mixer fitted with the whisk attachment. Beat on medium-high speed until pale and foamy, 3 to 5 minutes. Gradually add ½ cup sugar, beating until very pale and fluffy, 5 to 7 minutes. Add oil in a steady stream, beating to incorporate. Add the orange zest and lemon zest; beat 1 minute.

3. Reduce speed to medium low. Alternately add the flour mixture and the citrus juices, a little of each at a time, beginning and ending with flour mixture. Set batter aside.

4. In a clean mixing bowl, whip the egg whites on low speed until foamy. Add cream of tartar, and increase speed to medium high. Beat until soft peaks form. Gradually add the remaining ¼ cup sugar; beat until whites are glossy and stiff peaks form, about 1½ minutes. Stir one quarter of the whites into the batter. Fold in the remaining whites, being careful not to deflate the batter.

5. Gently pour the batter into an ungreased 7-inch tube pan. Bake until cake is golden brown and a cake tester inserted into middle comes out clean, about 40 minutes. Remove cake from oven. Invert pan, and let cake cool completely. Run a knife between cake and sides of pan; remove outer part of pan. Run a knife between cake and tube, and remove tube. Turn cake upside-down onto a cardboard cake round. Using a serrated knife, slice cake into three layers.

6. Spread half of the lemon-curd filling over the bottom layer. Top with a second cake layer, and spread with remaining filling. Top with third cake layer. Chill assembled cake until set or overnight. Brush off excess crumbs with a dry pastry brush.

7. Heat oven to 400°. Using an icing spatula, spread the Swiss meringue all over the cake, making decorative swirls. Place cake, still on cake round, on an oiled baking sheet. Transfer to oven. Bake, watching carefully, until meringue has browned around edges and begins to brown elsewhere. Transfer cake to a serving plate, and serve.

lemon-curd filling | **makes 1½ cups**

4 large egg yolks
2 large whole eggs
¾ cup sugar
½ cup freshly squeezed lemon
 juice plus grated zest from
 2 lemons
4 tablespoons unsalted butter,
 cut into small pieces

This tart lemon curd adds a pleasing sharpness to the delicate chiffon cake and sweet, fluffy meringue.

1. In a small, heavy-bottomed saucepan, whisk together the egg yolks and whole eggs. Add the sugar and lemon juice. Set over low heat, and cook, stirring constantly, until mixture coats the back of a wooden spoon, 8 to 10 minutes. Remove pan from heat, and stir to cool slightly.

2. Strain curd through a sieve set over a small bowl. Add the butter, a piece at a time, stirring until smooth after each addition. Stir in the lemon zest, and let cool completely.

swiss meringue | **makes enough for one 7-inch cake**

5 *egg whites*
³/₄ *cup sugar*
1 *teaspoon pure vanilla extract*

Warming the egg whites dissolves the sugar and gives this meringue greater volume.

1. Combine the egg whites, sugar, and vanilla in the heat-proof bowl of an electric mixer. Set the bowl over a pan of simmering water. Whisk constantly until the sugar has dissolved and whites are hot to the touch, 5 to 7 minutes.

2. Transfer the bowl to the electric mixer. Using the whisk attachment, mix on low speed, gradually increasing to high speed, until stiff, glossy peaks form, about 10 minutes. Use immediately.

5 warm chocolate cakes

14 *ounces best-quality*
    bittersweet chocolate
6 *tablespoons heavy cream*
6 *tablespoons unsalted butter,*
    plus more for baking rings
5 *large eggs, separated*
10 *tablespoons sugar*
½ *teaspoon pure vanilla extract*
³/₄ *cup ground almonds*
    Confectioners' sugar,
    for dusting (optional)

These single-portion cakes are baked in metal baking rings. You can bake as few as you like at one time; just keep the extras, wrapped tightly in plastic, in the freezer until ready to bake. | **makes 6 individual cakes**

1. Chop 2 ounces chocolate into small pieces, and place in a small bowl. Pour the cream into a small saucepan, and set over medium heat. Cook until bubbles appear around the edges. Pour the hot cream over the chocolate, and let stand several minutes; stir until smooth. Pour the ganache into six squares of a plastic ice-cube tray. Freeze until solid.

2. Line a baking sheet with parchment. Butter six 3-inch metal baking rings (see the Guide), and place the rings on the baking sheet. Set baking sheet aside.

3. Melt the butter and the remaining 12 ounces chocolate in a heat-proof bowl or the top of a double boiler over a pan of simmering water. Stir until smooth. Remove from heat, and let cool slightly.

4. Combine the egg yolks, 6 tablespoons sugar, and the vanilla in the bowl of an electric mixer. Beat until thick and pale yellow, 5 to 8 minutes. Add the warm chocolate-butter mixture, and combine thoroughly. Fold in the ground almonds.

5. In a separate bowl, beat the remaining 4 tablespoons sugar with the egg whites until stiff. Fold the egg whites into the chocolate mixture.

6. Spoon about 3 tablespoons batter into each ring. Remove frozen ganache cubes from freezer (dip the bottom of the ice-cube tray in a hot-water bath to release them, if necessary). Place a ganache cube in the center of each ring. Spoon the remaining batter into the rings, keeping the ganache cubes in the centers and covering them completely. Freeze filled molds until solid, about 1 hour.

7. Heat oven to 375°. Remove the baking sheet from the freezer. Transfer baking sheet to the oven, and bake until cakes have puffed slightly over the tops of the rings, 20 to 25 minutes. Transfer baking sheet to a wire rack; let cool, 5 to 10 minutes.

8. To unmold, cover one hand with a clean kitchen towel, and, using a spatula, pick cake up with the other hand. Invert cake into hand, pull off ring, then invert again onto a plate. Dust with confectioners' sugar, if desired. Serve warm cakes immediately.

6 *The flavor of this bittersweet-chocolate torte enveloped in a shiny chocolate glaze is most intense at room temperature. This cake is remarkably versatile—perfect after a casual meal or a formal dinner. Here a blown-glass plate and dome let the cake shine. The silver-plated knife is Victorian.*

6 chocolate-almond torte

1 cup (2 sticks) unsalted butter,
 cut into pieces, plus more for pan

8 ounces best-quality bittersweet
 or semisweet chocolate,
 chopped into pieces

5 large eggs, separated,
 room temperature

¼ cup dark-brown sugar

¾ cup granulated sugar

1 teaspoon pure vanilla extract

¼ cup ground almonds

½ cup cake flour (not self-rising)
 Pinch cream of tartar
 Shiny Chocolate Glaze
 (recipe follows)
 Silver dragées, for decorating

This torte is baked in a springform pan, which has a bottom that detaches from the sides and is used for cakes that cannot be inverted from a pan. Because the cake freezes well, it's great to have on hand for an impromptu dinner party: Wrap it tightly in plastic and foil; defrost it, then glaze. | **makes one 8-inch-round cake**

1. Heat oven to 375°. Butter an 8-inch springform pan; line the bottom with parchment paper. Butter the paper. Set the prepared pan aside.

2. Combine the butter and chocolate in a heat-proof bowl or the top of double boiler. Set over a pan of barely simmering water. Stir occasionally until melted and smooth. Remove pan from heat.

3. In the bowl of an electric mixer fitted with the whisk attachment, combine egg yolks, both sugars, and the vanilla. Stir in the warm chocolate mixture, ground almonds, and flour. Set aside.

4. Using a clean mixing bowl and beaters, beat the egg whites and the cream of tartar on medium speed until creamy. Increase speed to high, and beat until rounded peaks form.

5. Stir a quarter of beaten egg whites into reserved chocolate mixture; fold in the remaining whites.

6. Pour the batter into the prepared pan; smooth top. Bake until a cake tester inserted into middle comes out with moist crumbs sticking to it, 50 to 55 minutes. Transfer to a wire rack to cool completely.

7. Place a wire rack over a clean baking pan. Unmold the cake, and place on the rack. Ladle lukewarm glaze over the cake (below left), spreading glaze with bottom of ladle (below right). A perfect coat requires enough glaze so it flows generously over sides. If the first coat seems thin, add a second one after 30 minutes. Any glaze that collects in the pan can be scraped and reused. Decorate the center of cake with several silver dragées.

shiny chocolate glaze | **makes enough for one 8-inch-round cake**

For a perfect coat, the glaze should be just lukewarm when you coat the torte.

8 ounces bittersweet
 chocolate, chopped

8 tablespoons (1 stick)
 unsalted butter

1 tablespoon corn syrup

Place chocolate and butter in a heat-proof bowl or the top of a double boiler. Add corn syrup, and set over a pan of simmering water. Stir occasionally until melted and smooth. Use immediately.

7 citrus poppy-seed cake

1½ cups (3 sticks) unsalted butter, room temperature, plus more for pans

3¾ cups all-purpose flour, plus more for pans

2½ teaspoons baking powder

¾ teaspoon salt

2½ cups sugar

7 large eggs, lightly beaten, room temperature

1½ teaspoons pure vanilla extract

1 cup milk, room temperature

½ teaspoon grated lemon zest

½ teaspoon grated orange zest

½ teaspoon grated lime zest

⅓ cup poppy seeds, plus more for sprinkling

Shiny Cream-Cheese Frosting (recipe follows)

Lemon Glaze (recipe follows)

1 navel orange (optional)

1 lemon (optional)

So the glaze will be soft and glistening, apply it just before serving. | **makes one 8-inch-round layer cake**

1. Heat oven to 350°; arrange two racks in center of oven. Butter three 8-by-2-inch round cake pans; line each with a circle of parchment paper. Butter paper, and dust pans with flour; tap out excess. Set aside.

2. Sift together the flour, baking powder, and salt in a medium mixing bowl. Set aside.

3. In the bowl of an electric mixer fitted with paddle attachment, cream butter on medium-low speed until lightened, 1 to 2 minutes. Gradually add sugar; beat until color has lightened, 3 to 4 minutes, scraping down sides of bowl once or twice. Drizzle in eggs, a little at a time, beating on medium-low speed after each addition until batter is no longer slick but is smooth and fluffy, about 5 minutes. Stop to scrape down bowl once or twice so batter will combine well. Beat in vanilla on medium-low speed.

4. Reduce the mixer speed to low. Alternately add the reserved flour mixture and the milk, a little of each at a time, beginning and ending with the flour mixture. Scrape down the bowl once or twice. Beat in the lemon zest, orange zest, lime zest, and poppy seeds.

5. Divide batter evenly among the prepared pans. Bake 30 minutes, then rotate pans for even browning. Bake until a cake tester inserted into center of cakes comes out clean, 5 to 10 minutes more. Transfer to wire racks to cool, 15 minutes. Turn out cakes, and set on racks, tops up. Cool completely.

6. Remove parchment from bottom of each layer. Save prettiest layer for the top. Place one layer on the serving platter. Spread 1½ cups cream-cheese frosting over the top. Place second cake layer on top, and spread remaining 1½ cups frosting over top. Place reserved layer on top. Chill cake, loosely covered with plastic wrap, 1 hour.

7. When ready to serve, stir the lemon glaze well. Pour glaze over the center of the cake, and let it run down the sides. Using a single-hole zester, cut long strips of zest from the orange and the lemon, if desired. Arrange the zest in loose spirals on the top of cake, and sprinkle with poppy seeds.

shiny cream-cheese frosting | makes 3 cups

You will need to let this frosting chill for at least three hours before spreading.

12 ounces cream cheese, room temperature

6 tablespoons unsalted butter, room temperature

3 cups confectioners' sugar

1. In the bowl of an electric mixer fitted with the paddle attachment, beat cream cheese on medium-low speed until smooth, about 1 minute. Add the butter, and cream until smooth, about 2 minutes. Add the confectioners' sugar on low speed, and mix until completely combined.

2. Beat frosting on medium speed until smooth and fluffy, about 1 minute. Transfer to an airtight container, and chill until firm, 3 hours or overnight.

lemon glaze | makes ⅔ cup

This glaze may be made three to four hours ahead.

1½ cups confectioners' sugar

3 to 4 tablespoons freshly squeezed lemon juice

2 teaspoons poppy seeds

Place the sugar in medium bowl. Gradually add the lemon juice, stirring with a fork to combine until smooth. The mixture should be slightly thick; add another tablespoon lemon juice if necessary. Stir in the poppy seeds. Store, refrigerated, in an airtight container.

7 *Poppy seeds and bright flecks of citrus zest accentuate the fine crumb of this tender triplex cake. Two different icings complete the dessert: a cream-cheese frosting for richness between the layers, and a lemon glaze on top for a tart finish. Here, an unusual and refreshing clam-broth-glass cake stand is the perfect pedestal.*

8 *Caramel frosting is paired with tangy, bourbon-enhanced crème-fraîche filling on this three-layer ginger-pecan cake. The elegant pool of frosting is ringed with pecan halves and crystallized ginger. Unlike most cakes, this one should be refrigerated if it isn't eaten immediately; bring it to room temperature before serving.*

8 ginger-pecan cake

7 ounces pecans plus
nine pecan halves

1½ cups (3 sticks) unsalted butter,
room temperature, plus more
for pans

3 cups sifted all-purpose flour,
plus more for pans

1½ tablespoons baking powder

¾ teaspoon salt

1 tablespoon ground ginger

3 cups light-brown sugar, sifted

6 large whole eggs,
lightly beaten

1 cup plus 2 tablespoons milk

¾ teaspoon freshly grated ginger

2 teaspoons pure vanilla extract

1 pint crème fraîche

2 teaspoons bourbon (optional)

3 tablespoons confectioners'
sugar, or more to taste
Glossy Caramel Icing
(recipe follows)

¼ ounce crystallized ginger
(see the Guide), cut into
thin strips

If the layers of this cake seem to be slipping during assembly, anchor them with thin wooden skewers or toothpicks; just be sure to remove them before serving. | **makes one 8-inch-round layer cake**

1. Heat oven to 350°; arrange two racks in the center of oven. Spread all the pecans on a baking pan. Bake pecans until fragrant, and transfer to a bowl to cool. Reserve nine pecan halves, and finely grind the remaining nuts in a food processor, yielding 1½ cups.

2. Butter three 8-by-2-inch round cake pans; line each with a circle of parchment. Butter paper, and dust bottoms and sides of pans with flour; tap out any excess. Set pans aside.

3. In a medium bowl, sift together flour, baking powder, salt, and ground ginger. Add the ground pecans, and whisk to combine.

4. In the bowl of an electric mixer fitted with paddle attachment, cream butter until light and fluffy. Gradually add the brown sugar, and beat until fluffy, 4 to 5 minutes. Drizzle in the eggs, a little at a time, beating until batter is no longer slick, about 5 minutes; scrape down sides twice.

5. Reduce mixer speed to low. Alternately add flour mixture and milk to batter, a little of each at a time, starting and ending with flour mixture; scrape down bowl twice. Beat in grated ginger and vanilla.

6. Divide batter among the pans. Bake 30 minutes, then rotate pans for even browning. Bake until a cake tester inserted into center of cakes comes out clean, 5 to 10 minutes more. Transfer pans to wire racks to cool, 15 minutes. Turn out cakes, and return to wire racks to cool completely, tops up.

7. In bowl of electric mixer, whip crème fraîche until soft peaks form. Add bourbon, if using, and confectioners' sugar; beat until soft peaks return. Cover with plastic wrap; chill until firm, about 1 hour.

8. Remove parchment from bottoms of cakes. Set aside the prettiest layer for the top. Place one cake layer on serving platter; spread with half of the crème-fraîche filling. Place a second cake layer on top; spread with remaining filling. Top with reserved cake layer. Chill cake while preparing icing.

9. Pour caramel icing onto center; let flow down sides. Let icing set slightly, 5 to 10 minutes; arrange the pecan halves and crystallized ginger on the top. Cut with a knife dipped in hot water and wiped dry.

glossy caramel icing | **makes 1½ cups**

1½ cups sugar
¾ cup heavy cream

You'll need a candy thermometer to assess the readiness of this icing. Be careful not to let the sugar get too hot while melting; the hotter the caramel becomes, the more it hardens when cooling, making the cake more difficult to slice.

1. Place sugar in a large skillet, and set over medium heat. Cook until sugar begins to melt and turns golden, 2 to 3 minutes. Stirring with a wooden spoon, cook sugar until amber in color and a candy thermometer registers about 310°, 3 to 4 minutes.

2. Slowly stir in the cream, being careful to avoid splattering. Reduce the heat to medium low, and continue stirring; the hardened caramel will melt into the cream and become soft and liquid.

3. Using a whisk, stir slowly, minimizing bubbles, until completely smooth, 1 to 3 minutes. Remove pan from heat, and let cool, 3 to 4 minutes. Pour the icing directly onto the chilled cake. If the caramel becomes too stiff to pour, warm in a double boiler.

9 pecan torte with apricot filling

Unsalted butter, for pans
⅔ cup plus 1 tablespoon sifted
   cake flour (not self-rising),
   plus more for pans
1½ cups pecans
1½ teaspoons baking powder
½ teaspoon cinnamon
¼ teaspoon salt
6 large eggs, separated,
   room temperature
½ cup plus 2 tablespoons
   granulated sugar
1 teaspoon pure vanilla extract
1¾ cups chunky apricot preserves
½ cup dried apricots
   Confectioners' sugar,
   for decorating

A drum-shaped nut grinder is the best tool for grinding pecans. You can also use a food processor; add one tablespoon flour, and process in pulses. The flour keeps the nuts from becoming oily. | **makes one 9-inch-round cake**

1. Heat oven to 350°. Butter and flour a 9-inch springform pan. Spread pecans on a baking pan, and bake until aromatic, 5 to 6 minutes. Transfer to a bowl to cool, then grind into a fine powder. Place powder in a large bowl; add flour, baking powder, cinnamon, and salt.

2. In the bowl of an electric mixer fitted with whisk attachment, beat egg yolks with half of the granulated sugar until the mixture is thick and pale and holds a ribbonlike trail on the surface for 1 second when you raise the beaters. Beat in the vanilla, and set batter aside.

3. In a clean bowl, whip egg whites until they just hold stiff peaks. Add the remaining granulated sugar; beat until stiff peaks form again.

4. Stir 1 cup egg whites into the batter. Place one-fourth of the remaining egg whites on top, and sprinkle one-fourth of the flour-nut mixture over the top. Fold in quickly. Repeat adding whites and flour-nut mixture in this way until both have been incorporated.

5. Pour the batter into the prepared pan, and bake until a cake tester inserted into the middle comes out clean, about 35 minutes. Transfer to a wire rack to cool, 10 minutes. Unmold the cake, and set on wire rack, top up, until completely cool.

6. Place the apricot preserves in medium saucepan. Set over low heat, and cook until warm to the touch. Place the dried apricots in another saucepan, and cover with water. Bring to a simmer, and cook until softened. Using a slotted spoon, transfer apricots to the warm preserves; stir to combine.

7. Using a serrated knife, slice cake horizontally into two layers. Place one layer on a serving platter. Spoon whole apricots and 1½ cups warm preserves over cake layer; top with second cake layer. Strain remaining preserves; brush liquid over sides. Decorate with confectioners' sugar (below).

stenciling polka dots *Trace the circumference of the cake pan on a large sheet of paper. 1. Trace a pattern of circles using a drinking glass about two inches in diameter. Cut out circles with a utility knife. 2. Lay stencil over cake. Put some confectioners' sugar in a sieve, and tap sugar over the cake until circles are covered. 3. Remove stencil, then tap a lighter layer of sugar over the entire surface.*

9 *This pecan torte is made from a single layer that is sliced in two and filled with apricot preserves; polka dots are made of confectioners' sugar dusted on top. Because there is no frosting or filling to prepare, this is an easy cake. Its playful design and fruity, nutty flavor make it a perfect ending for a Sunday brunch.*

10 Ripe peaches, sweet and juicy, are the very essence of summer. This icebox cake makes them even more tantalizing: Four almond meringues are layered with mascarpone cream and peach purée, then topped with caramelized peaches. On a warm day, this chilled dessert is just the right confection after a dinner of grilled fish and salad. The scallop-edged cake stand is English nineteenth-century ironstone.

10 peach icebox cake

2 1/3 cups whole almonds, blanched
   or unblanched
1 cup granulated sugar
6 large egg whites
   Pinch of salt
1 cup mascarpone cheese
1 cup heavy cream
3 tablespoons confectioners' sugar
1 teaspoon pure vanilla extract
1 tablespoon peach schnapps
   Peach Caramel Sauce
   (recipe follows)

Blanched almonds produce a more finely textured, lighter colored cake. | **makes one 8-inch-round layer cake**

1. Heat oven to 350°. Cut two 12-by-16-inch rectangles out of parchment. Using a pencil, trace two 8-inch circles on each piece of parchment. Place parchment, pencil sides down, on two baking sheets.

2. Combine the almonds and all but 1 tablespoon granulated sugar in the bowl of a food processor. Pulse until fine, about 1 minute. Transfer almond mixture to a large bowl.

3. In the bowl of an electric mixer fitted with the whisk attachment, beat egg whites and salt until soft peaks form, about 1 minute. Add remaining tablespoon granulated sugar; beat 30 seconds more.

4. Fold one-third of the egg whites into the almond mixture until well combined. Fold in the remaining egg whites until just incorporated.

5. Divide batter evenly among four traced circles. Using an icing spatula, spread mixture to edges of circles. Transfer baking sheets to oven; bake until cakes are lightly browned and a tester inserted into the middle comes out clean, 20 to 25 minutes; rotate baking sheets twice while baking. Transfer to wire racks to cool, 3 minutes. Remove parchment; return cakes to racks until completely cool.

6. Combine mascarpone cheese, heavy cream, confectioners' sugar, and vanilla in the bowl of the electric mixer. Beat with the whisk attachment, beginning at low speed and increasing to medium high, until mixture is thick and fluffy, about 1 1/2 minutes. Transfer to the refrigerator.

7. Place one cake layer right-side up on a serving platter. Brush top lightly with peach schnapps. Spoon one-fourth of the mascarpone cream on top; spread to within 1/2 inch of edge. Spread a third of the peach purée (reserved from step four in caramel peach sauce, below) over the cream. Repeat process twice, assembling two more layers. Place the fourth cake layer on top; press down gently so mascarpone cream and peach purée flow to edges. Brush top of cake with remaining peach schnapps, and spread remaining mascarpone cream over top. Insert four or five toothpicks into top of the cake; lay plastic wrap over the top, covering cake without touching it. Chill 1 hour or overnight.

8. When ready to serve, remove plastic wrap and toothpicks. Lift peach pieces out of sauce, and arrange on top of cake. Serve remaining sauce on the side, or spoon over individual slices.

peach caramel sauce | **makes 3 cups**

4 large ripe peaches
   (about 1 1/3 pounds)
3/4 cup sugar

1. Bring a medium saucepan of water to a boil, and have ready an ice-water bath. Cut an "x" in the bottom of each peach, and place peaches in boiling water. Cook until skins loosen, 1 to 2 minutes. Using a slotted spoon, transfer peaches to the ice-water bath to stop cooking process. Remove skins from peaches, and cut in half. Discard pits, and slice each half into 6 wedges.

2. Combine sugar and 1/2 cup water in a small saucepan. Cover, and cook over medium-high heat until sugar has completely dissolved, 3 to 4 minutes. Remove cover, and reduce heat to medium low. Cook until the sugar turns medium amber, about 15 minutes. While cooking, wipe down sides of pan several times with a pastry brush dipped in cold water to prevent crystals from forming.

3. Working quickly, remove pan from heat; stir in peach slices with a wooden spoon. Return pan to heat; continue cooking caramel, stirring occasionally, until peaches are soft, about 5 minutes.

4. Remove pan from heat, and let cool slightly. Transfer half of the peach caramel to a medium bowl; set aside. Transfer the remaining half to a food processor; purée until smooth, about 30 seconds. Return half of the purée to the peach caramel, and reserve the remaining purée (about 3/4 cup) for brushing over the cake (step seven, above). Cover peach caramel with plastic wrap; chill until using.

11 *Only the graham-cracker crust of this little cheese-cake needs to be baked. Ricotta and orange zest make the cake light and citrusy; a candied blood-orange slice set in a sheer blood-orange glaze decorates the top. Blood oranges usually appear in markets in December and are available through early spring.*

11 blood-orange cheesecake

2 cups ricotta cheese

¾ cup graham-cracker crumbs
(6 or 7 crackers)

¾ cup sugar

4 tablespoons unsalted
butter, melted

3 tablespoons freshly squeezed
lemon juice

1 packet unflavored gelatin

4 large egg yolks

½ cup plus 2 tablespoons milk
Pinch of salt
Grated zest of ½ orange

1 teaspoon pure vanilla extract

4 ounces cream cheese,
room temperature

½ cup heavy cream, whipped

1 Candied Blood-Orange Slice
(recipe follows)
Blood-Orange Glaze
(recipe follows)

You'll need to chill this cheesecake overnight in the springform pan; begin draining the ricotta at least several hours or the day before before preparing the cake. | **makes one 7-inch-round cake**

1. Line a sieve with cheesecloth, and place over a bowl. Put the ricotta in the cheesecloth, and let drain in the refrigerator several hours or overnight.

2. Heat oven to 350°. Line the bottom of a 7-inch springform pan with parchment paper. Combine the graham-cracker crumbs and 2 tablespoons sugar in a small bowl. Using a fork, stir in the butter until crumbs are moist. Press mixture into bottom of the pan, and bake 10 minutes.

3. Place lemon juice in a small bowl, and sprinkle gelatin over the surface. Let soften 10 minutes.

4. In a small, heavy saucepan, beat egg yolks until smooth. Whisk in milk. Gradually whisk in remaining sugar and salt. Cook over low heat, stirring constantly, until mixture coats the back of a wooden spoon, about 7 minutes, being careful not to boil. Transfer to a bowl; stir.

5. Stir in the softened gelatin, the orange zest, and the vanilla. Mix until the gelatin has completely dissolved, and set the custard aside.

6. Place drained ricotta in bowl of a food processor; purée until smooth. Add cream cheese; process again until smooth. With machine running, add warm custard, pulsing to combine. Transfer mixture to a bowl; fold in whipped cream. Pour mixture into prepared pan. Cover, and chill overnight.

7. Place the candied orange slice in center of cake (below). Pour lukewarm blood-orange glaze over top, tipping cake pan to cover completely. Chill until glaze has set, about 1 hour.

8. To unmold, wrap a damp, hot kitchen towel around sides of pan; run a thin knife between cake and pan. Carefully unmold, and slide onto a serving plate.

candied blood-orange slices | makes 5 or 6

1 blood orange, scrubbed

¾ cup sugar

2 tablespoons light corn syrup

You'll only need one slice to decorate the cake, but making several allows you to choose the prettiest.

1. Cut orange into ⅛-inch-thick rounds. In a small saucepan set over medium heat, combine the sugar, 2 cups water, and corn syrup. Bring to a boil. Cover, and simmer until the liquid is clear and no crystals cling to pan, about 3 minutes. Add the orange rounds in one layer. Simmer until transparent, about 1 hour.

2. Transfer rounds to a wire rack to cool.

blood-orange glaze | coats one 7-inch cake

7 tablespoons freshly squeezed
blood-orange juice
(2 oranges), strained

¾ teaspoon unflavored gelatin

2 tablespoons sugar

¼ teaspoon cornstarch

1. Place 2 tablespoons orange juice in a bowl. Sprinkle gelatin over top. Let stand until soft, about 10 minutes.

2. Combine the sugar and 4 tablespoons orange juice in a small saucepan, and bring to a boil. Combine the remaining tablespoon orange juice and cornstarch in a small bowl. Stir until dissolved; whisk into boiling orange juice. Remove from heat. Stir in softened gelatin. Cool until lukewarm.

12 *It's hard to imagine a better way to end a Christmas feast than with this delightfully gooey Bartlett pear and ginger-bread upside-down cake. Here, it is surrounded with Forelle pears that have been caramelized; any small pears, such as Seckel, would also work well. We tucked sprigs of verbena all around, but you can use any greenery that is non-toxic and hasn't been sprayed.*

13 *Our applesauce cake— wet, dense, and spiced with ground cinnamon, nutmeg, cloves, and ginger—is more like a fruitcake than the traditional light dessert cake. It is especially good on a crisp autumn morning with a cup of freshly brewed black coffee.*

12 pear upside-down cake

10 tablespoons butter, room
    temperature, plus more for pan
5 large ripe Bartlett pears,
    peeled, cored, and quartered
2 tablespoons freshly squeezed
    lemon juice
4 tablespoons granulated sugar
6 tablespoons brandy
1 cup all-purpose flour
1 tablespoon ground ginger
1 teaspoon ground cinnamon
¼ teaspoon ground cloves
¼ teaspoon ground nutmeg
¼ teaspoon salt
¼ cup packed dark-brown sugar
3 large eggs
½ cup unsulfured molasses
1 tablespoon freshly
    grated ginger
1 teaspoon baking soda

When you invert this cake, rearrange the pears, if necessary. | **makes one 9-inch-square cake**

1. Heat oven to 350°. Butter a 9-inch-square cake pan, and set aside.

2. In a large bowl, toss pears with lemon juice. In a large skillet set over medium-high heat, melt 2 tablespoons butter; sprinkle with 2 tablespoons granulated sugar. Add half of the pears, cut-sides down, in a single layer; cook until brown on bottoms, 2 to 3 minutes. Turn pears over; cook other cut sides until brown, 2 to 3 minutes. Transfer to a plate. Repeat with remaining pears.

3. Add brandy to pear juices remaining in skillet; sprinkle remaining 2 tablespoons granulated sugar over liquid. Cook, stirring, until reduced to syrup, about 1 minute. Pour into pan; swirl to coat. Starting in one corner, fan out pears in single layer; arrange tapered sides in same direction. Set pan aside.

4. In a medium bowl, whisk together the flour, ground ginger, cinnamon, cloves, nutmeg, and salt.

5. In bowl of an electric mixer, cream remaining 8 tablespoons butter until fluffy. Add brown sugar; beat on medium-high speed for 3 minutes. Add eggs; beat to combine. Beat in molasses and grated ginger. Add half of flour mixture; combine on low speed. In a small bowl, combine baking soda and 2 tablespoons boiling water; beat into batter. Beat in the remaining flour mixture until combined.

6. Pour batter into pan; bake 25 minutes. Reduce heat to 325°; bake until springy to the touch, 15 to 20 minutes. Cool on wire rack, 1 hour. Run a knife between cake and pan, and invert onto a serving plate.

13 applesauce cake

4 ounces pecans
1 cup (2 sticks) plus 3 tablespoons
    unsalted butter, room tempera-
    ture, plus more for pan
2¼ cups superfine sugar
2 large eggs
2½ cups applesauce
2¾ cups plus 3 tablespoons
    all-purpose flour
1½ teaspoons ground cinnamon
½ teaspoon ground nutmeg
    Pinch of ground cloves
    Pinch of salt
1¾ teaspoons baking powder
1 teaspoon pure vanilla extract
2 tablespoons Calvados
    or brandy
1 large apple, peeled and
    very thinly sliced (1 cup)
¼ cup light-brown sugar
¼ teaspoon ground ginger

Because of its moistness, this cake keeps exceptionally well in the refrigerator and improves with time. Resist eating it fresh out of the oven because the flavor reaches its peak the next day. | **makes one 10-inch-round cake**

1. Heat oven to 350°. Spread the pecans on a baking sheet, and bake until toasted and aromatic. Transfer to a bowl to cool. Reduce oven temperature to 325°. Chop pecans, yielding 1 cup.

2. Brush a 10-inch springform pan with butter. Coat with ¼ cup superfine sugar; lightly tap out any excess. Set the prepared pan aside.

3. In the bowl of an electric mixer fitted with the paddle attachment, combine 1 cup butter and remaining 2 cups superfine sugar. Beat on medium speed, scraping down sides with a rubber spatula, until mixture is light and fluffy, about 5 minutes. Add eggs, one at a time, beating 1 full minute after each addition. Fold in the applesauce, being careful not to overmix.

4. In a large bowl, sift together 2¾ cups flour, 1 teaspoon cinnamon, ¼ teaspoon nutmeg, the cloves, the salt, and the baking powder.

5. Fold the flour mixture and chopped pecans into the applesauce mixture. Add the vanilla, the Calvados, and the apple slices, and mix until just combined. Transfer the batter to the prepared pan.

6. Combine the remaining 3 tablespoons butter, 3 tablespoons flour, ½ teaspoon cinnamon, ¼ teaspoon nutmeg, brown sugar, and ginger in a small mixing bowl. Mix with fingers until just combined; sprinkle lightly over the batter. Place pan in oven; bake until a cake tester inserted into center comes out clean, about 1 hour 50 minutes. Transfer to a wire rack to cool completely. Unmold before serving.

14 cranberry upside-down cake

12 tablespoons unsalted butter,
   room temperature, plus
   more for pan
¾ cup all-purpose flour,
   plus more for pan
2¾ cups fresh or frozen
   cranberries, thawed
9 tablespoons pure maple syrup
½ teaspoon ground cinnamon
1 teaspoon baking powder
¼ teaspoon salt
6 tablespoons yellow cornmeal,
   preferably coarse
¼ cup almond paste
¾ cup plus 2 tablespoons sugar
3 large eggs, separated
¼ teaspoon pure vanilla extract
¼ teaspoon pure almond extract
½ cup milk

In many homes, cranberries show up but just once a year. Think beyond cranberry sauce; take advantage of this fruit's tart, distinctive flavor to make an old-fashioned upside-down cake. This almond-flavored cake is baked on top of cranberries that have been simmered in maple syrup and flavored with cinnamon. When the cake is turned out of its pan, the cranberries make a dramatic topping. Because fresh cranberries freeze so well, right in the bag, this cake can be made any time of year. Serve it plain for breakfast or for dessert at night with a scoop of vanilla ice cream. **| makes one 8-inch-round cake**

1. Butter and flour an 8-inch round cake pan; set aside.

2. In a large skillet, heat 6 tablespoons butter over medium heat until it sizzles. Add cranberries, and cook until they are shiny, 2 to 3 minutes.

3. Add the maple syrup and cinnamon. Cook, stirring frequently, until cranberries soften but still hold their shapes, about 5 minutes.

4. Using a slotted spoon, transfer the cranberries to a baking sheet, and let cool slightly. Set the skillet containing the syrup aside.

5. Arrange cranberries in the prepared pan. Return skillet with syrup to medium heat, and cook until syrup comes to a boil, 3 to 4 minutes. Immediately pour syrup over cranberries; let cool, 10 minutes.

6. Heat oven to 350°; position rack in center of oven.

7. In a large bowl, sift together flour, baking powder, and salt. With a fork, mix in cornmeal. Set aside.

8. Place the remaining 6 tablespoons butter in the bowl of an electric mixer fitted with the paddle attachment. Crumble in the almond paste, and beat on medium speed until well combined, about 30 seconds. Gradually add ¾ cup sugar, and beat until creamy. Add the egg yolks, and beat until well combined. Beat in the vanilla and almond extracts. In two batches, alternately add the flour mixture and milk. Set the batter aside.

9. In a clean bowl of the electric mixer fitted with the whisk attachment, beat egg whites until foamy. Slowly add the remaining 2 tablespoons sugar; beat until soft peaks form. Whisk one-third of the egg whites into the batter, then fold in the remaining whites.

10. Spread the batter over the cranberries in the pan, and bake until a cake tester inserted in center comes out clean, about 45 minutes. Transfer cake to a wire rack to cool, 2 hours. Invert cake onto a serving plate, and serve.

15 tiramisu wedding cake

For the cake layers (1 batch):

  Unsalted butter, for pans
  All-purpose flour, for pans
3½ cups whole blanched almonds
1 tablespoon baking powder
8 large eggs, room temperature
2 cups sugar

For assembling:

  Kirsch, for drizzling
2½ recipes Mascarpone Filling
  (recipe follows)
10½ pints mixed seasonal berries,
  such as red and golden raspberries, fraises des bois, and
  red currants
  Confectioners' sugar
  Berries on the vine and wild
  rose hips, or other unsprayed
  nontoxic vines or branches

You will need to prepare three-and-a-half batches of cake batter to make the three fourteen-inch layers, three eleven-inch layers, and three eight-inch layers needed to assemble this cake; one batch of batter makes one fourteen-inch cake and one eleven-inch cake; a half-batch makes three eight-inch cakes. | **serves 75 to 80**

1. Heat oven to 350°. Brush baking pans with butter. Line with parchment, butter again, and dust with flour. Tap out any excess.

2. Place almonds and baking powder in bowl of food processor, and pulse until just finely ground, being careful not to overprocess. Set aside.

3. Place eggs and sugar in heat-proof bowl of an electric mixer, and stir to incorporate. Place bowl over a pan of simmering water, and whisk constantly until the sugar has dissolved, about 10 minutes.

4. Return bowl to mixer fitted with the whisk attachment. Beat on medium-high speed until light and fluffy, about 7 minutes. Lift whisk from mixture, and draw a figure eight by dripping batter from attachment; when pattern remains on the surface for 3 seconds, batter is ready.

5. Using a rubber spatula, gently fold almond mixture into batter. Fill each pan with ½ inch of batter. Bake until golden, 20 to 25 minutes; the centers will rise and fall during baking. Transfer pans to a wire rack; let stand 5 minutes. Turn out cakes onto corresponding cardboard rounds. Peel off parchment, and invert onto another round; cakes will be right-side up. Let cool completely; wrap in plastic.

6. Wrap the top halves of eight 7-inch-tall spike support pillars with floral tape. Place one 14-inch cake layer right-side up on a Masonite round. Drizzle kirsch over the top. Spread 3 cups mascarpone filling over top, and sprinkle with 1 pint of berries. Dollop 1 cup of filling over berries. Dust a 14-inch cardboard round with confectioners' sugar (to help cakes slide off cardboard; sugar again as necessary). Place a 14-inch layer on sugared round, and slide layer, without cardboard, onto first layer; press lightly. Repeat with kirsch, mascarpone filling, and berries. Slide a third 14-inch layer on top. Sift confectioners' sugar over the cake.

7. Attach 4 support pillars to a 10-inch separator plate. Press supports through the assembled 14-inch layers. Smear 2 tablespoons filling over separator. Slide one 11-inch cake layer off cardboard onto separator. Drizzle kirsch over cake. Spread 2 cups filling over kirsch, and sprinkle with ½ pint of berries. Dollop 1 cup filling on top. Slide another 11-inch layer on top, and repeat the filling process. Slide third 11-inch layer on top. Press slightly, and sift with confectioners' sugar.

8. Attach 4 spike support pillars to a 7-inch separator plate. Press supports through the assembled 11-inch layers. Smear 2 tablespoons filling over the separator. Slide one 8-inch cake layer off cardboard and onto separator. Drizzle kirsch over cake. Spread 1 cup filling over kirsch, and sprinkle with just under ½ pint berries. Dollop ½ cup filling on top. Slide another 8-inch layer on top, and repeat filling process. Slide third 8-inch layer on top. Press slightly, and sift with confectioners' sugar.

9. Decorate cake with vines and branches; sprinkle each tier with another pint of raspberries.

mascarpone filling

2 cups heavy cream
1 cup confectioners' sugar
3 tablespoons kirsch
2 pounds mascarpone cheese,
  preferably Galbani, left at
  room temperature 15 minutes

1. Have ready two large ice-water baths, and chill the bowl of an electric mixer.

2. Combine the cream and sugar in the chilled bowl, and whip until firm peaks form, about 3 minutes. Set bowl in an ice-water bath to chill.

3. Set a large bowl in the other ice-water bath. Add the mascarpone, and whisk until smooth. Whisk in the kirsch and half of the whipped cream; fold in the remaining cream. Chill until ready to use.

15 *Instead of a traditional frosting, the jewel-like berries of summer — raspberries, fraises des bois, red currants — are strewn over this fanciful wedding cake. Chewy almond wafers are stacked with mascarpone cream and golden raspberries, then garnished with berry brambles and wild-rose hips. You can make the cake layers the day before, then make the filling and assemble the cake on the day of the wedding. Plastic separators, readily available at baking-supply stores, make assembling the cake relatively easy.*

16 *Baked and served in the fruits' own shells, these lemon soufflés require five ingredients: lemons, eggs, flour, sugar, and an ounce of care — an essential element to any soufflé. Regular lemons work fine, but if you are lucky enough to find Meyer lemons, use them. Smooth, sweet, and fragrant, they will make this airy confection a little more special. Choose those lemons with the prettiest and most consistent rinds.*

chapter two

Spoon Desserts

Casual or elegant,
they are the sweet,
smooth favorites
that define comfort and bliss

Even though they are easy to make using readily available ingredients, spoon desserts tend to be eclipsed by fancier confections. And that's a pity. Spoon desserts—puddings, gelatins, even a warm fruit crumble—are wonders of texture, offering the enjoyment of something smooth and flavorful cavorting on your tongue, touching every single taste bud. Even more subtle is the pleasing rhythm of eating with a spoon—where we all began as children. ✻ Consider one of the simplest spoon desserts: bread pudding. Leftover bread is baked in milk, eggs, and flavoring. The result, a custardy French toast, is a food so comforting it practically demands pajamas. Dense and sweet, steamed or baked, apple or cranberry or chocolate, our other warm puddings make gentle endings to winter meals and Christmas feasts. When the weather is warm, however, try our summer pudding, a chilled dessert made of bread and juicy berries. ✻ For another cool comfort, revisit the gelatin parfait. Our sophisticated version is layered with espresso gelatin and both coffee and vanilla panna cotta, a custardlike dessert. We've rediscovered the appeal of gelatins, with an emphasis on fresh, natural flavors more suited to today's tastes. The technique is simple: Powdered unflavored gelatin is softened in cold liquid; then hot, but not boiling, liquid is stirred in. Then, of course, the dessert must set in the refrigerator. To shape ours, we used ramekins, a terrine mold, and a vintage gelatin mold. Be imaginative, and experiment with different containers—many classic or unusual molds can be found at tag sales. Because these pretty gelatins can be prepared ahead of time without ever turning on the oven, they are perfect for summer entertaining. ✻ Puddings and gelatins are both so open to variation—you can make them from almost anything, in almost any shape. That's the essence of a spoon dessert: the melding of simple ingredients into a comforting dessert, to be scooped up effortlessly and with great pleasure.

16 little lemon soufflés

8 large lemons, preferably Meyer
3 large eggs, separated
½ cup granulated sugar
2 tablespoons all-purpose flour
Confectioners' sugar,
for dusting

Use a melon baller or serrated grapefruit spoon to scoop out the rinds. | **serves 8**

1. Heat oven to 350°; line a baking sheet with parchment. Trim tip end from a lemon so fruit sits level. Cut stem end one-third of the way down, making cut parallel with bottom; reserve top. Repeat.

2. Hold a lemon above a sieve set over a bowl, and scoop out the pulp. Squeeze the juice from the pulp, and reserve. Repeat with all lemons. Place shells on prepared baking sheet.

3. Combine egg yolks, ¼ cup granulated sugar, ¼ cup reserved lemon juice, and flour in the heat-proof bowl of an electric mixer fitted with the whisk attachment. Beat mixture on medium speed until pale yellow, about 3 minutes. Place bowl over a pan of simmering water; whisk constantly until very thick, about 8 minutes. Remove bowl from heat, and return to mixer. Beat on medium speed until cool, scraping down sides several times, about 10 minutes. Transfer to a medium bowl, and set aside.

4. Combine egg whites and remaining ¼ cup granulated sugar in clean mixer bowl. Place the bowl over the pan of simmering water, and stir until sugar has dissolved and mixture is warm to the touch. Remove bowl from heat, and return to mixer; beat on low speed until frothy. Gradually increase speed until meringue is shiny and holds soft peaks, 2 to 3 minutes, being careful not to overbeat.

5. Whisk one-third of the meringue into the yolk mixture. Gently fold in the remaining meringue. Carefully fill the prepared lemon shells to just below the rims.

6. Transfer baking sheet to oven, and bake until meringue is slightly golden and rises about one inch above the shell, about 14 minutes. Remove from oven, and transfer to serving plates. Garnish with the reserved lemon tops, and dust with confectioners' sugar. Serve immediately.

17 summer-fruit crumble

1 cup plus 1½ tablespoons
all-purpose flour
½ cup packed dark-brown sugar
½ teaspoon cinnamon
Pinch of salt
½ cup rolled oats
10 tablespoons unsalted butter,
chilled and cut into small pieces
4 nectarines (about 1¾ pounds),
peeled, pitted, and cut into
one-inch chunks
2 mangoes (about 1½ pounds),
peeled, pitted, and cut into
one-inch chunks
1 pint raspberries
½ cup granulated sugar
2 tablespoons freshly squeezed
lime juice

This simple summer dessert is irresistible served warm with a dollop of vanilla ice cream. | **serves 10 to 12**

1. Heat oven to 375°. In the bowl of an electric mixer fitted with the paddle attachment, combine 1 cup flour, brown sugar, cinnamon, salt, and oats. Mix on low speed 30 seconds. Add the butter, and mix until clumps form, 4 to 5 minutes. Transfer topping to a bowl. Cover, and refrigerate until using.

2. Place nectarine and mango chunks in a large bowl. Add raspberries. Add remaining 1½ tablespoons flour, granulated sugar, and lime juice; toss gently.

3. Transfer the fruit to a shallow 12-inch-round gratin dish. Distribute the reserved topping evenly over fruit.

4. Bake until the topping is golden brown and the juices bubble, about 50 minutes. Transfer to a wire rack to cool slightly. Scoop into dishes, and serve warm.

18 *This café gelatin is especially dazzling in a tall glass wine goblet. Two layers—one vanilla and one espresso—of rich panna cotta, a sensuous Italian dessert whose name means "cooked cream," sandwich a thin layer of espresso gelatin. Garnishing the top are pieces of espresso gelatin.*

18 café gelatin

3 cups heavy cream
9 tablespoons sugar
1 tablespoon finely ground
  espresso
3¼ teaspoons powdered
  unflavored gelatin
1¼ cups strong brewed espresso,
  chilled
¼ vanilla bean, split

Layered desserts are much easier to prepare than they look, but they do take some time. For this dessert, each layer must be made and chilled before the next one is added, so the flavors and colors won't run together. You'll need to start about four hours before serving time, or you can make it a full day ahead. | **serves 6**

1. Combine ¾ cup cream, 3 tablespoons sugar, and ground espresso in a saucepan set over medium-low heat. Stir until dissolved. Bring just to a boil, and remove from heat. Let steep 5 minutes.

2. Pour ¾ cup cream into the top half of a double boiler. Sprinkle 1 teaspoon gelatin over cream, and let stand until softened, about 5 minutes.

3. Add the warm espresso mixture. Place mixture over a pan of simmering water. Whisk until gelatin has dissolved, 3 to 5 minutes. Strain espresso panna cotta through a cheesecloth-lined sieve set over a bowl. Pour ¼ cup espresso panna cotta into each of six tall 8-ounce glasses. Cover with plastic, and refrigerate until set, about 1 hour.

4. Place ½ cup brewed espresso in a bowl. Sprinkle 1¼ teaspoons gelatin over liquid, and let stand until softened, about 5 minutes.

5. Combine the remaining ¾ cup brewed espresso and 3 tablespoons sugar in a saucepan, and set over medium-low heat. Bring just to a boil; remove from heat. Add to espresso-gelatin mixture, and whisk to dissolve. Let espresso gelatin cool to room temperature. Add 2 tablespoons to each serving glass. Cover, and refrigerate until set, about 40 minutes. Transfer the remaining espresso gelatin to a small baking dish; cover, and refrigerate until set.

6. Combine ¾ cup cream and remaining 3 tablespoons sugar in a saucepan. Scrape the vanilla seeds into the cream, and add the pod. Bring just to a boil. Remove from heat, and let steep 5 minutes.

7. Pour the remaining ¾ cup cream in the top of a double boiler. Sprinkle the remaining 1 teaspoon gelatin over the top, and let stand until softened, about 5 minutes.

8. Pour the hot cream over the gelatin mixture, and set over a pan of simmering water. Whisk until the gelatin dissolves, 5 minutes. Pour vanilla panna cotta through a cheesecloth-lined sieve; let cool to room temperature. Pour ¼ cup into each serving glass. Cover, and refrigerate until set, 1½ hours.

9. Just before serving, cut the reserved espresso gelatin into cubes, and spoon on top of vanilla layer.

19 *This buttermilk panna cotta has the texture of an ethereal custard. It is served with strawberries in a statuesque Venetian glass; the graceful underplate is rose glass. Before serving, sprinkle the strawberries with a bit of sugar to draw out their natural juices.*

20 *A slice of lemon terrine is served with lemon confit, mint leaves, mint syrup, and a scoop of lemon sorbet on an early-twentieth-century octagonal green-glass plate. The terrine, which is unmolded on a platter before being sliced, is a wonderfully refreshing mix of clean, clear flavors that will delight anyone who loves the taste of lemon.*

19 buttermilk panna cotta with strawberries

2 cups nonfat buttermilk

1½ teaspoons powdered
   unflavored gelatin

⅔ cup heavy cream

¾ cup sugar

1 pint strawberries, hulled
  and quartered

For a more casual presentation, you can chill the panna cotta in one large bowl instead of individual ramekins, but it will take longer to set; use a serving spoon or an ice-cream scoop to serve it with fresh berries. | **serves 6**

1. Pour 1 cup buttermilk into top half of a double boiler; sprinkle gelatin over top. Let stand until softened, about 5 minutes. Place six 4-ounce ramekins, small bowls, or custard cups on a baking sheet.

2. Combine the cream and a scant ½ cup sugar in a small saucepan, and bring to a boil.

3. Add cream mixture to gelatin mixture. Place over a pan of simmering water. Whisk until gelatin has dissolved, about 5 minutes. Stir in remaining cup buttermilk. Pass mixture through a cheesecloth-lined sieve. Divide among ramekins; cover with plastic wrap. Refrigerate until set, about 4 hours.

4. Place strawberries in a medium bowl; sprinkle remaining ¼ cup sugar over tops. Let stand 1 hour.

5. When ready to serve, unmold by dipping ramekins briefly into a hot-water bath and running tip of a knife around edges. Invert onto serving plates or into bowls; garnish with strawberries and juice.

20 lemon terrine

1¾ cups freshly squeezed lemon
    juice (about 12 lemons)

4 packets powdered
  unflavored gelatin

3¼ cups sugar

8 to 10 individual mint leaves
  plus 1 cup packed leaves

3 lemons, sliced into ¼-inch-
  thick rounds

To make this dessert, you will need to use a four-cup porcelain terrine mold or an enameled cast-iron terrine mold (see the Guide). | **serves 8 to 10**

1. Place 1 cup lemon juice in a bowl. Sprinkle gelatin over top; let stand until softened, about 5 minutes.

2. Combine 1 cup sugar and 3½ cups water in a saucepan. Bring to a boil, and stir, until sugar has dissolved. Pour syrup over gelatin mixture; whisk to dissolve gelatin. Add remaining ¾ cup lemon juice.

3. Pour ⅓ cup gelatin mixture into terrine mold. Cover gelatin with 8 to 10 mint leaves, pressing leaves into the gelatin. Cover with plastic wrap. Refrigerate until set, 45 to 50 minutes.

4. Add the remaining gelatin mixture. Cover with plastic wrap; refrigerate until firm, about 4 hours.

5. Heat oven to 300°. Arrange lemon slices in a single layer in the bottom of a glass baking dish. Combine 1¼ cups sugar and 1 cup water in a small saucepan; bring to a boil, stirring to dissolve the sugar. Pour over lemons. Bake until translucent, about 45 minutes. Let lemon confit cool.

6. Combine remaining cup sugar and ¼ cup water in a saucepan; bring to a boil over high heat, stirring to dissolve sugar. Let cool to room temperature. Transfer syrup to refrigerator.

7. Bring a pan of water to a boil, and have ready an ice bath. Blanch 1 cup mint leaves in boiling water 30 seconds. Drain in a colander, and transfer to ice bath. Drain; squeeze in a kitchen towel to dry.

8. Purée chilled syrup and mint leaves in a blender. Strain through a fine sieve; chill mint syrup 1 hour.

9. To serve, unmold terrine by dipping it briefly into a hot-water bath and running the tip of a knife around edge. Invert terrine onto a platter; serve individual slices with lemon confit and mint syrup.

21 caramel-apple steamed pudding

½ cup plus 2 ½ tablespoons
 granulated sugar

4 Granny Smith apples, peeled,
 cored, and cut into
 one-inch chunks

½ teaspoon ground cinnamon

½ teaspoon ground ginger

¼ teaspoon ground nutmeg

¼ teaspoon ground cloves

9 tablespoons unsalted butter

½ cup brown sugar

2 large eggs

¼ cup molasses

1 ¼ cups all-purpose flour

2 ¼ teaspoons baking powder
 Pinch of salt

1 cup bread crumbs

Make this pudding in a two-quart lidded metal pudding mold. Coat the mold with caramel (below left) before you add the caramelized apples and dense batter. When unmolded (below right), the caramelized apples become a glistening topping. | serves 8 to 10

1. Combine ½ cup granulated sugar and 1 tablespoon water in a small, heavy saucepan; set over medium heat. Cover, and cook until the sugar has melted. Remove cover, and continue cooking, swirling pan occasionally, until sugar turns a deep amber. Carefully pour caramel into pudding mold; tip so caramel coats mold evenly. Set mold aside.

2. Place half of the apple chunks in a small saucepan, and add 2 tablespoons water, 1½ table-spoons granulated sugar, the cinnamon, the ginger, the nutmeg, and the cloves. Place saucepan over low heat, and cook, covered, until the apples fall apart, 10 to 12 minutes. Uncover, and cook 5 minutes more, stirring often. Set the applesauce aside.

3. Melt 1 tablespoon butter in a small sauté pan; add the remaining apple chunks and the remaining 1 tablespoon granulated sugar. Cook over medium-high heat until apples turn brown on all sides, 3 to 5 minutes. Place apples in the bottom of the mold, distributing evenly so they reach up the sides.

4. Choose a pot large enough to hold the pudding mold with a 2-inch space all around. Place a wire rack or a folded kitchen towel in the bottom of pot; fill with enough water to reach halfway up sides of mold. Cover pot, and bring to a boil. Reduce heat to a simmer.

5. In the bowl of an electric mixer, cream together 8 tablespoons butter and brown sugar. Add the eggs and molasses; mix well. Add the reserved applesauce, and mix well.

6. In a large bowl, sift together the flour, baking powder, and salt; stir in the bread crumbs. Add to the applesauce mixture. Stir batter until just combined.

7. Fill pudding mold with batter; clamp on lid. Place mold in pot of simmering water. Cover pot, and cook until a toothpick inserted into middle of pudding comes out clean, about 1 hour 40 minutes. Check water often, keeping it at a steady, low simmer. Transfer mold to a wire rack to cool, 15 minutes.

8. When ready to serve, invert the pudding onto a serving plate. If any of the apple chunks stick to the mold, remove them, and rearrange them on the top; slice.

22 pumpkin bread pudding

1 small sugar pumpkin or
   or 1 cup canned pumpkin
   Unsalted butter, room
   temperature, for dishes
2 large whole eggs, lightly beaten
1 large egg yolk, lightly beaten
1 cup milk
1 tablespoon unsulfured molasses
¼ cup sugar
1 teaspoon pure vanilla extract
½ teaspoon ground ginger
½ teaspoon ground cinnamon
   Pinch of salt
1 heaping cup ½-inch cubes fresh
   brioche or white bread
   Caramel Sauce (recipe follows)

This pudding works well with either fresh or canned pumpkin. If you use fresh, the best choice is a sugar pumpkin—you can also use a butternut squash. | **serves 6**

1. Heat oven to 350°. Cut the pumpkin in half, and remove seeds and strings. Fill a glass baking dish with ¼ inch water. Place the pumpkin, cut sides down, in dish. Bake until tender when pierced with a fork, about 40 minutes. Remove pumpkin from pan, and let cool. Scoop out flesh, and purée in a food processor or blender. Measure out 1 cup, and set aside. Freeze remaining purée for another use.

2. Reduce heat to 325°. Butter six 4-ounce ramekins or custard cups, and set aside.

3. In a medium bowl, whisk together pumpkin purée, whole eggs, egg yolk, milk, molasses, sugar, vanilla, ginger, cinnamon, and salt.

4. Divide the bread cubes among the ramekins, and pour the pumpkin mixture over the bread. Let sit until the bread has absorbed the liquid, about 10 minutes.

5. Place the ramekins in a roasting pan, and pour in enough boiling water to reach halfway up the sides. Bake until puddings are brown and centers have set, about 40 minutes. Let cool, 10 minutes.

6. Turn individual puddings out onto dessert plates; spoon the caramel sauce around each pudding.

caramel sauce

1 cup sugar
2 tablespoons freshly squeezed
   lemon juice

1. Combine the sugar and lemon juice in a small saucepan, and set over medium heat. Cover, and cook until the sugar has melted, 6 to 8 minutes. Have ready an ice bath. Remove cover, and continue cooking, swirling pan occasionally, until sugar turns a deep-amber color.

2. Plunge the bottom of the pan into a bowl of cold water to stop the cooking process. Wearing oven mitts, carefully pour in ½ cup hot water, being careful that the caramel doesn't splatter. Stir until incorporated, and set aside until ready to use.

22 *Pumpkin bread pudding is the kind of dessert thrifty cooks appreciate — it needs only some leftover bread and ingredients found in the pantry and refrigerator. Put the small puddings in the oven at the start of dinner, and they'll be ready for dessert. Served on an engraved glass soup plate and bathed in caramel sauce, each one is as elegant as it is homey.*

23 *Dotted with dried cranberries, topped with ribbons of candied orange zest, and served with cranberry coulis, these baked semolina puddings make a wonderful winter-holiday dessert. A pair of Venetian champagne glasses holds these pretty puddings aloft. The spoons are George II–period sterling silver.*

24 *The stark beauty of a chocolate sponge pudding is enhanced by a nineteenth-century Sèvres footed dish. As it bakes, the pudding separates into two layers, one creamy and smooth, the other more cakey and spongy, making this a spoon dessert you may choose to eat with a fork.*

23 cranberry-semolina pudding

4 cups milk
1 vanilla bean, split lengthwise
Zest of 1 orange
½ cup sugar
1 cup couscous
3 large egg yolks
1 teaspoon baking soda
1 cup dried cranberries
Cranberry Coulis
(recipe follows)
Candied orange zest (see the
Guide), for garnish

Couscous is a tiny pasta made from semolina. | **makes 8 individual puddings or 1 large pudding**

1. Butter eight 4-ounce ramekins or one 7-cup pudding mold or bowl; set aside.

2. In a medium saucepan set over medium heat, bring the milk to a boil. Add the vanilla bean, orange zest, and sugar. Remove pan from heat, and cover. Let stand 30 minutes. Discard vanilla bean.

3. Return mixture to a boil over medium heat. Stir in the couscous. Return mixture to a simmer, and cook 10 minutes. Remove pan from heat, and cover. Set aside until couscous absorbs all liquid, about 15 minutes.

4. Heat oven to 350°. Add the egg yolks, baking soda, and cranberries; stir to combine. Divide batter among ramekins, and place them in a roasting pan. Pour boiling water into roasting pan so it comes halfway up sides of ramekins.

5. Bake until puddings are set, 35 to 40 minutes. Add boiling water as necessary to maintain water level. Set aside to cool slightly.

6. When ready to serve, invert puddings onto serving plates. Top with the cranberry coulis, and garnish with candied orange zest.

cranberry coulis | **makes 1 cup**

1½ cups fresh cranberries
⅓ cup sugar
Zest of 1 orange

Place cranberries, sugar, orange zest, and ¾ cup water in a small saucepan. Set over medium heat, and bring to a boil. Reduce heat to a simmer; cook until cranberries have popped, about 12 minutes. Pass coulis through a sieve, and discard solids. Chill until serving.

24 chocolate sponge pudding

½ cup hazelnuts
2 tablespoons unsalted butter,
plus more for bowl
8 tablespoons sugar
Pinch of salt
2 tablespoons all-purpose flour
1 teaspoon cocoa powder
¾ cup milk
2½ ounces bittersweet chocolate,
broken into small pieces
2 large eggs, separated
1 teaspoon pure vanilla extract

Serve this warm pudding from the bowl, or cool it slightly and invert it onto a plate. | **serves 4 to 6**

1. Heat oven to 350°, Spread hazelnuts over a baking sheet, and toast until fragrant. Transfer nuts to a bowl to cool. Roughly chop; set aside. Reduce temperature to 325°. Butter a 5-cup pudding bowl.

2. In a large bowl, combine 5 tablespoons sugar with salt, flour, and cocoa powder. Set aside.

3. Pour the milk into a medium saucepan, and scald.

4. Combine the chocolate and butter in a heat-proof bowl, and melt over a pan of simmering water. Pour the scalded milk over the chocolate-butter mixture.

5. In bowl of electric mixer, beat yolks. Stir a little warm chocolate mixture into yolks to temper. Add yolks to chocolate mixture. Add vanilla; stir until combined. Stir chocolate mixture into flour mixture.

6. Beat egg whites and remaining 3 tablespoons sugar until stiff; fold into batter. Pour batter into pudding bowl; place on a rack in a roasting pan. Pour boiling water into pan halfway up sides of bowl. Bake until pudding has set, 40 to 45 minutes. Add boiling water to pan to maintain water level.

7. Let pudding cool slightly in the bowl, and garnish with the toasted hazelnuts.

25 champagne gelatin with peaches and plums

3 cups rosé champagne

3½ cups sugar

6 chamomile tea bags (or ⅓ cup loose tea)

6 peaches

2 packets powdered unflavored gelatin

2 plums, cut in half and pits removed

We used a fancy mold to give this gelatin its triple-tiered shape; a pale-yellow compote displays it gracefully. You can also use a four- or five-cup Bundt pan for this dessert. | **serves 8**

1. Place champagne, 2 cups sugar, tea bags, and 6 cups water in a large saucepan. Set over high heat, and bring to a boil. Reduce heat, and simmer 10 minutes.

2. Add peaches, and gently simmer until a knife pierces peaches easily, 5 to 20 minutes. Set aside to cool, about 3 hours.

3. Peel peaches. Slice 2 of the peaches into eighths, and set remaining peaches aside. Strain liquid. Transfer 2 cups liquid to a medium bowl, and chill. Reserve remaining poaching liquid.

4. Sprinkle gelatin over chilled liquid; let stand until softened, about 5 minutes.

5. Bring 2 cups of the reserved poaching liquid to a boil. Add to gelatin mixture; whisk until gelatin dissolves, about 5 minutes. Pour 3 tablespoons mixture into mold, coating the bottom. Cover; chill until just set, about 30 minutes.

6. Combine remaining 1½ cups sugar and 1½ cups poaching liquid in a skillet; bring to a boil, stirring to dissolve sugar. Reduce heat to a simmer. Add plums, cut-sides down, and poach until skins loosen, 5 to 10 minutes. Remove pan from heat.

7. Transfer plums to a bowl, and remove skins. Slice each into 4 wedges, and chill.

8. Arrange plums on top of gelatin in mold. Add ¾ cup gelatin mixture. Cover with plastic, and refrigerate until set, about 45 minutes.

9. Add remaining gelatin; arrange peach slices on top. Cover with plastic; chill until set, about 6 hours.

10. When ready to serve, unmold by dipping mold briefly into a hot-water bath and running the tip of a knife around edge. Invert onto a platter. Cut reserved peaches in half, and discard pits. Serve gelatin with the peach halves.

26 summer pudding

1 pint strawberries, hulled and
   sliced ¼-inch thick
¾ cup granulated sugar
1 pint blueberries
1½ pints raspberries
½ pint blackberries
2 tablespoons freshly squeezed
   lemon juice
   Pinch of salt
18 slices white bread
1 cup heavy cream
1 teaspoon pure vanilla extract
1 tablespoon confectioners' sugar

In this dessert, layers of bread are saturated with berry juice, so it is important to use a firm, good-quality white sandwich bread; otherwise, the pudding may not stand up. | **serves 6**

1. Combine strawberries and granulated sugar in a large straight-sided skillet, and set over medium heat. Cook until strawberries release their juices and sugar has dissolved, about 5 minutes. Add blueberries, raspberries, and blackberries; cook until they release their juices but still hold their shape, about 5 minutes; the mixture will look like a thick soup. Remove from heat, and transfer to a mixing bowl to cool. Stir in the lemon juice and the salt.

2. Line six ½-cup ramekins with plastic wrap. Cut a circle from each slice of bread the same diameter as a ramekin; you will have 18 circles.

3. Spoon 2 tablespoons of the berry mixture into each ramekin. Dip 6 of the bread circles, one at a time, into the bowl of berries, saturating bread. Place saturated bread in the ramekins. Cover with 2 tablespoons berry mixture. Continue layering process, ending with a layer of bread, brimming over tops of ramekins. (If you need more juice, press remaining berries through a coarse sieve.)

4. Arrange ramekins in a shallow baking pan, and cover with plastic wrap. Place a board large enough to cover them all on top. Weight the board with heavy cans (about 5 pounds); chill overnight.

5. When ready to serve, combine cream, vanilla, and confectioners' sugar in a chilled metal bowl; whip until stiff but soft peaks form, 2 to 3 minutes. Remove the top layer of plastic wrap, and invert the puddings onto individual dessert plates; remove the ramekins and remaining plastic wrap. Top with a dollop of whipped cream.

26 *One summer-long pleasure is carrying home pint after pint of ripe berries. This summer pudding, a beloved traditional dessert in England, is made of layers of bread and juicy strawberries, blueberries, raspberries, and blackberries. The berries are cooked very briefly, but the pudding, once assembled, is not; instead, it is compressed and chilled overnight in the refrigerator. Vanilla-flavored whipped cream caps the dessert, which is served here in an ironstone soup plate.*

27 *Just a little bit of craftsmanship updates a holiday tradition. Part pumpkin pie, part pumpkin flan, this poised little dessert has a caramel sauce and a traditional pâte-brisée shell and is served with a dollop of crème fraîche. The flan is refrigerated overnight, then inverted into place before serving.*

chapter three

Pies &
Tarts

Follow a few basic tips,
and a perfectly flaky,
tender crust will always be
your lovely reward

Pie and tart making is a surprisingly relaxing pursuit. So many foods can become great fillings, from the rarest berries to a humble autumn squash. The process of filling a pie invites you to experiment—to toss in some raisins, just to see what happens, or maybe add some cinnamon. You can play with proportions or make substitutions with a freedom you don't have when baking a cake. But the payoff is just as grand. A pie will suffuse your house with delicious, soothing aromas that last for hours—maybe longer than the pie. ✳ Nothing could be easier than a pie, so long as you master the crust. For some reason, however, a lot of people are afraid of making a pie shell. The many brands of prepared ones in supermarket freezers suggest that the filling is easy, and the crust a mystery. But making a successful one is primarily just a matter of keeping the ingredients well chilled. In a food processor, you can make a good dough in less than a minute. Once prepared, refrigerate it for an hour, so it will be easy to roll out. Whenever you're rolling or cutting dough, work in a cool kitchen and, if you can, on a cool surface like marble—if the dough is too warm, it gets sticky. ✳ Piecrusts can be made with lard or vegetable shortening, but our favorite, a traditional French crust called pâte brisée, uses butter. It is consistently flaky and tender. Some of our tarts use a slightly sweeter version called pâte sucrée. And there are other crusts: Our chocolate-pecan pie has a chocolate crust; our fig tart, a cornmeal crust. ✳ Of course, just as pie making can be plain, it can also be fanciful. Cut out leaves from the dough to decorate the top, or punch little holes to create a lattice. You can even dispense with the pie tin altogether and experiment with baking individual pies in ovenproof cups or other little containers, as we did to make our wonderfully eccentric eggnog cups. ✳ So go on—get out your cherries, and apples, and figs, and nuts, and all the other ingredients that beg to be put in a pie, and start rolling.

27 pumpkin flan in pastry shell

2¾ cups sugar

2¼ cups milk

1½ cups canned pumpkin purée

2 teaspoons freshly grated ginger

¼ teaspoon freshly grated nutmeg

½ teaspoon ground cinnamon

¾ teaspoon salt

5 large whole eggs

2 large egg yolks

2 teaspoons pure vanilla extract
All-purpose flour, for
rolling out dough
Pâte Brisée (recipe follows)

1 cup whipped cream or crème
fraîche (optional)

If you do not use the exact sizes of the pans called for in this recipe, just be sure that they are close to these sizes and that the pastry shell you make is slightly larger than the custard. | **makes eight 4-inch flans**

1. Have ready eight 4-inch metal pie pans, and prepare an ice-water bath.

2. In a small saucepan, combine 2 cups sugar and 1 cup water; set over medium-high heat. Cook, stirring, until sugar has dissolved. Cover, and bring to boil; cook until condensation washes down sides. Remove cover; boil until syrup turns deep amber in color. Quickly submerge pan in ice-water bath.

3. Working quickly, divide caramel among the pie pans; swirl each to coat bottom. Set aside to cool.

4. Heat oven to 325°. Pour milk into a saucepan, and set over high heat. Bring just to a boil; set aside.

5. In a large bowl, combine pumpkin purée, remaining ¾ cup sugar, ginger, nutmeg, cinnamon, salt, whole eggs, and egg yolks. Mix in vanilla and warm milk; pass through fine sieve, discarding solids. Divide mixture among pie pans, filling two-thirds full. Transfer pie pans to a roasting pan, and add enough boiling water to the roasting pan to come halfway up sides of pie pans.

6. Loosely drape piece of foil over top of roasting pan, and transfer to oven. Bake until centers are nearly set—a thin-bladed knife inserted into centers should come out clean—60 to 65 minutes. Transfer roasting pan to wire rack to cool. Remove flans from water, and dry bottoms of pie pans. Cover with plastic wrap, and refrigerate flans overnight.

7. Heat oven to 375°. Have ready four 5-inch flan rings or fluted tartlet tins (see the Guide); line two baking sheets with parchment. On a lightly floured surface, roll out pâte brisée to an ⅛-inch thickness. Cut out eight 7-inch circles. Ease a circle into each flan ring, letting excess drape over top. Fit dough into bottom corners of rings, using knuckles to work dough from top down, not from the center out. Using a rolling pin, roll over tops of rings, creating neat tops and removing any excess dough. Prick bottom of each shell several times with a fork. Transfer shells to baking sheets, and chill 30 minutes.

8. Line shells with foil, and fill with pie weights or dried beans. Bake 20 minutes, and remove foil and weights. Bake until shells are golden brown, 2 to 4 minutes more. Transfer baking sheets to a wire rack, and let shells cool, 1 hour. Remove shells from rings.

9. When ready to serve, place the shells on four dessert plates. Unmold flan by running a knife carefully around edge of pan, and invert it over a shell; caramel sauce will flow, filling shell. Repeat with remaining shells and flan. Top with whipped cream or crème fraîche, if desired.

pâte brisée | **makes 1 pound, 5 ounces**

Pâte brisée is the French version of classic pie or tart pastry. Pressing the dough into a disk rather than shaping it into a ball allows it to chill faster and more thoroughly; it will also be easier to roll out. If you freeze it, the flatness will allow it to thaw more quickly.

2½ cups all-purpose flour

1 teaspoon salt

1 teaspoon sugar

1 cup (2 sticks) unsalted butter,
chilled and cut into small pieces

1. In the bowl of a food processor, combine flour, salt, and sugar. Add the butter, and process until the mixture resembles coarse meal, 8 to 10 seconds.

2. With machine running, add ¼ cup ice water in a slow, steady stream through feed tube. Pulse until dough holds together without being wet or sticky; be careful not to process more than 30 seconds. To test, squeeze a small amount together: If it is crumbly, add more ice water, 1 tablespoon at a time.

3. Divide dough into two equal balls. Flatten each ball into a disk, and wrap in plastic. Transfer to the refrigerator, and chill at least 1 hour. Dough may be stored, frozen, up to 1 month.

29 plum tart

Pâte Sucrée (recipe, page 62), chilled

3 *tablespoons almond paste (see the Guide)*

1 *tablespoon all-purpose flour*

1¼ *pounds (4 or 5) Santa Rosa plums, pitted and sliced into ¼-inch-thick wedges*

2 *teaspoons sugar*

1 *large egg yolk*

1 *tablespoon heavy cream*

¼ *cup plum or red-currant jam*

Almond paste and Amanda Rosa plums, an aromatic and firm-fleshed variety grown in California's Sierra Nevada, are used in this rustic, elongated, rectangular tart. Any firm, ripe plum will work well. If you prefer, you can make the same recipe in a nine-inch-round tart ring. | **makes one 4½-by14-inch tart**

1. Heat oven to 375°. Line a baking sheet with parchment paper, and set a 4½-by-14-inch bottomless tart form on top. Set the baking sheet aside.

2. On a clean work surface, roll out pâte sucrée to a 7½-by-17-inch rectangle, about ⅛ inch thick. Roll the rectangle onto pin; unroll over form; let extra dough hang over edge. Using knuckles, fit dough into form.

3. Crumble the almond paste evenly over the dough, and sprinkle the flour evenly over the almond paste. Arrange the sliced plums in a fish-scale pattern on top of the dough; sprinkle the plums with the sugar.

4. Fold overhanging dough over plums; tear, creating a 1-inch free-form edge. Transfer the baking sheet to the refrigerator; chill dough 10 to 15 minutes.

5. In a small bowl, combine the egg yolk and cream; beat lightly. Brush chilled pastry with egg wash.

6. Bake until crust is golden brown and fruit bubbles, about 35 minutes. Transfer tart to a wire rack.

7. In a small saucepan, combine the jam and 2 tablespoons water. Set pan over medium heat, and cook until warm. Remove pan from heat, and pass the glaze through a sieve; discard any solids. Brush the warm glaze over the plums in the tart. Let glaze cool slightly, remove tart form, and serve.

30 summer fruit tart

4 cups plus 3 tablespoons
   all-purpose flour
1 teaspoon salt
½ cup plus 2 teaspoons sugar,
   plus more for sprinkling
¾ pound (3 sticks) unsalted butter,
   chilled and cut into pieces
6 plums or peaches, pitted and
   sliced into ½-inch-thick pieces
4 to 5 pints fresh berries
   Milk, for brushing

We used a paella pan to make this tart of plums, peaches, and a mix of blackberries and raspberries. But it's easy to improvise with a recipe like this: A twelve-inch pizza pan also works well, and you can vary the kinds of fruit you use, depending on what happens to be at its peak. | **makes one 12-inch tart**

1. In the bowl of an electric mixer fitted with paddle attachment, combine 4 cups flour, salt, 2 teaspoons sugar, and half of the butter. Mix on medium speed until the mixture resembles coarse meal, about 3½ minutes. Add remaining half of the butter and 1 cup ice water; mix 20 seconds. Dough will be full of butter chunks. Turn out dough, and flatten into a 1-inch-thick disk. Wrap in plastic, and chill at least 1 hour.

2. Heat oven to 375°. In a large bowl, toss plums and peaches, if using, with 3 tablespoons flour and ½ cup sugar. Add berries, and gently toss.

3. On a lightly floured surface, roll out dough 4 inches larger than pan; transfer dough to pan. Arrange fruit in pan; fold dough toward center. Brush with milk; sprinkle with sugar. Bake 30 to 40 minutes, until fruit bubbles and crust is brown. Transfer to a wire rack to cool. Serve warm or at room temperature.

31 rustic cherry tart

All-purpose flour, for
   rolling out pastry
1 sheet frozen puff pastry,
   from standard package
   (17¼ ounces), thawed
5 tablespoons unsalted butter,
   room temperature
⅓ cup plus 4 teaspoons sugar
½ cup blanched almond
   flour (see the Guide)
1 large whole egg
½ teaspoon pure almond extract
1 large egg yolk
1 tablespoon heavy cream
1 pound red cherries, picked
   over, stemmed and pitted

Blanched almond flour is available in some specialty food stores. Or you can make your own with a food processor by grinding whole, blanched almonds as finely as possible. | **makes 1 nine-inch tart**

1. Heat oven to 425°. Line a clean work surface with parchment; sprinkle lightly with all-purpose flour. Roll out pastry to an ⅛-inch thickness. Cut a 12-inch circle from dough. Roll up edges, making a 10-inch crust. Transfer parchment and crust to a baking sheet; chill until firm, about 30 minutes.

2. Place the butter, ⅓ cup sugar, the almond flour, the whole egg, and the almond extract in a medium bowl; mix until well combined.

3. Prick entire surface of chilled crust with a fork. In a small bowl, combine the egg yolk and heavy cream; brush mixture on the surface and edges of the crust. Using an offset spatula, spread the almond mixture evenly in an ⅛-inch-thick layer over bottom of the crust, and chill 15 minutes more.

4. Spread the cherries in a single layer over the almond mixture. Bake tart 15 minutes.

5. Sprinkle remaining 4 teaspoons sugar over tart; continue baking until edges turn deep-golden brown, 5 to 10 minutes. Transfer to a wire rack to cool. Serve the tart warm or at room temperature.

31 *A trio of rustic, free-form tarts filled with fresh red cherries cools on a round breadboard. Ideal for a summer picnic, these flaky nine-inch tarts are much easier to transport — and neater to eat — than gooey cherry pies.*

32 *This stunning and
sophisticated tart is filled with
sweetened crème fraîche and
cream cheese, then topped with
fresh ripe figs. A cornmeal crust
is the perfect foil for the figs,
which are brushed with a glaze
made of red-currant jam and red
wine. If you like, make this tart
ahead of time, and refrigerate
for several hours before serving.*

32 fig tart with cream-cheese filling

*Cornmeal Tart Dough
(recipe follows)*

*4 ounces cream cheese,
room temperature*

½ cup crème fraîche

1½ tablespoons confectioners' sugar

*1 pint black or purple figs,
stemmed and quartered*

¼ cup fig or red-currant jam

*2 tablespoons red wine
Vegetable-oil cooking spray*

Cornmeal dough is a little harder to roll out than regular dough because it's more crumbly, but it's also easier to patch. Chill at least thirty minutes, until firm, and it will be easier to handle. | **makes one 4½-by-14-inch tart**

1. Coat a 4½-by-14-inch rectangular fluted tart tin with cooking spray. Place the cornmeal dough between two pieces of plastic wrap, and roll out to an ⅛-inch thickness. Discard the top piece of plastic, and gently invert dough over tin. Discard the remaining piece of plastic wrap. Using your fingers, press the dough into tin, and trim dough flush with edges. Repair any tears or cracks by pressing dough together with fingers. Chill crust 30 minutes.

2. Heat oven to 350°. Prick the chilled crust several times with a fork, and bake until the crust begins to take on color, 15 to 20 minutes. Remove from oven, and transfer to a wire rack to cool completely. When cool, remove from the pan, and transfer to a serving platter.

3. Place the cream cheese in the bowl of an electric mixer, and beat until smooth. Add the crème fraîche and confectioners' sugar; beat until mixture is smooth and fluffy, about 2 minutes. Transfer cream-cheese filling to refrigerator, and chill 30 minutes.

4. Spread the filling into the cooled crust, and arrange the figs on top, pressing them down slightly.

5. Combine the jam and wine in a small saucepan. Set pan over medium-high heat, and bring liquid to a boil, stirring frequently. Reduce heat, and simmer until mixture is thick and syrupy, about 2 minutes. Let glaze cool slightly. Using a pastry brush, brush glaze over the figs. Serve.

cornmeal tart dough | makes shell for one 4½-by-14-inch tart

*6 tablespoons unsalted butter,
room temperature*

½ cup sugar

2 large egg yolks

1 cup all-purpose flour

*⅓ cup yellow cornmeal,
preferably stoneground*

½ teaspoon salt

1. In the bowl of an electric mixer fitted with the paddle attachment, cream together the butter and sugar, about 2 minutes. Add the egg yolks, and mix just to combine.

2. In a large bowl, whisk together flour, cornmeal, and salt.

3. Add flour mixture to yolk mixture, and mix just until dough comes together loosely. Flatten dough into a disk, and wrap in plastic. Chill dough until firm, at least 30 minutes.

33 mini lemon-meringue pies

Basic Pie Dough (recipe follows)
2 cups sugar
6 tablespoons cornstarch
½ cup freshly squeezed
   lemon juice plus 2 tablespoons
   grated lemon zest (about 4
   lemons)
5 large whole eggs, separated
   Salt
4 tablespoons unsalted butter,
   cut into pieces
2 large egg whites

Snowdrifts of meringue top these individual lemon pies, which are perfect for those who love the crust even more than the filling. You can also make this recipe as one large pie: Use a nine-inch pie pan and half of the pie dough; freeze remaining dough for a later use. To crimp edges, use the thumb and forefinger of one hand to hold the dough on one side, then push with the thumb of the other hand to create a decorative edge; or use the thumb and forefinger of one hand to hold the dough while pressing down and in with the tines of a fork. | **makes six 4½-inch pies**

1. Heat oven to 400°. On a lightly floured surface, roll out the dough to an ⅛-inch thickness. Cut dough into six 7-inch diameter circles; place each circle in a 4½-inch pie pan. Crimp edges, and refrigerate until firm, about 30 minutes. Remove from refrigerator, and prick the bottoms of the shells with a fork.

2. Line shells with aluminum foil; fill with pie weights or dried beans. Transfer shells to oven; bake until the edges begin to turn brown, about 10 minutes. Remove foil and weights. Continue baking until golden brown, about 7 minutes. Transfer to a wire rack to cool.

3. In a medium bowl, sift together 1¼ cups sugar and the cornstarch. Stir in 2 cups water, and mix until smooth; set aside.

4. In a nonreactive saucepan, combine the lemon juice, 5 egg yolks, and a pinch of salt. Set over medium heat. Stir in the cornstarch mixture; cook, stirring constantly, until mixture comes to a boil, about 14 minutes. Remove from heat, and stir in the lemon zest and butter. Pour the filling into a bowl, and set aside to cool, stirring occasionally.

5. Pour lemon filling into the six piecrusts. Cover, and refrigerate until firm, about 1 hour.

6. Heat broiler. Combine 7 egg whites, the remaining ¾ cup sugar, and ¼ teaspoon salt in the heatproof bowl of an electric mixer. Hold the bowl over a pan of simmering water; whisk until the mixture is warm to the touch and the sugar has dissolved, about 3 minutes.

7. Return bowl to mixer, and beat until stiff peaks form. Using an offset spatula, spread each pie with meringue so the filling is covered and the meringue reaches the edges of the piecrusts. Transfer pies to broiler, and lightly brown the meringue, watching constantly, 30 to 45 seconds. Remove from broiler, and place on a wire rack to cool to room temperature. Serve.

basic pie dough | **makes crusts for six 4½-inch pies**

2½ cups all-purpose flour
1 teaspoon salt
2 teaspoons sugar
15 tablespoons unsalted butter,
   chilled and cut into pieces
3 tablespoons vegetable shortening

In the bowl of a food processor, combine the flour, salt, and sugar. Add the butter and the shortening; pulse until mixture resembles coarse meal. Add ¼ cup ice water in a slow, steady stream through the feed tube, pulsing, until mixture holds together. If necessary, add more ice water, 1 tablespoon at a time, until dough holds together when squeezed. Form dough into a ball; cover with plastic wrap. Flatten into a disk; refrigerate at least 1 hour.

34 baked-apple dumplings

For the dough:

2½ cups all-purpose flour

1 teaspoon salt

2 tablespoons sugar

½ pound unsalted butter (2 sticks), chilled and cut into small pieces

For the syrup:

¼ cup packed light-brown sugar

2 cups clear apple juice

2 tablespoons honey

½ cup Armagnac or brandy

¼ cup pure maple syrup

1½ teaspoons freshly grated ginger

2 tablespoons unsalted butter

2 tablespoons freshly squeezed lemon juice

For the filling:

2 tablespoons Armagnac or brandy

2 tablespoons dried cherries, roughly chopped

2 tablespoons all-purpose flour

2 tablespoons finely ground blanched almonds

2 tablespoons light-brown sugar

1 tablespoon unsalted butter, room temperature

⅛ teaspoon ground nutmeg

⅛ teaspoon ground mace

⅛ teaspoon ground cinnamon

4 McIntosh apples

1 lemon, cut into quarters lengthwise

4 cinnamon sticks

To assemble dumplings:

All-purpose flour, for rolling out dough

1 large egg white, lightly beaten

1 large egg yolk

1 tablespoon heavy cream

Baked apples are an old-fashioned autumn favorite; wrapping them like dumplings transforms each one into an individual pie. | **makes 4**

1. Place flour, salt, and sugar in bowl of a food processor; pulse 2 to 3 times to mix. Add butter; process until mixture resembles coarse meal, about 10 seconds. With machine running, add 4 to 6 tablespoons ice water in a steady stream through feed tube; process just until mixture begins to hold together, no more than 30 seconds. Flatten dough into a disk, and wrap in plastic. Chill dough at least 1 hour.

2. Combine all syrup ingredients in a medium saucepan. Cook over medium-high heat until liquid has reduced by half and has slightly thickened, about 20 minutes. Remove from heat; set syrup aside.

3. Combine Armagnac and cherries in a small bowl; let sit 20 minutes. Drain cherries, reserving Armagnac; add Armagnac to reserved syrup. In another small bowl, combine cherries, flour, ground almonds, brown sugar, butter, nutmeg, mace, and cinnamon; mix filling well with a wooden spoon.

4. Peel apples; remove stems and top three-quarters of core, leaving ¼ inch intact at bottom. Rub each apple with a lemon quarter to prevent discoloration. Divide filling among four apples, filling cavities. Insert a cinnamon stick into each cavity. Wrap exposed end of cinnamon stick with a piece of heavy-duty aluminum foil. Set filled apples aside.

5. Heat oven to 450°. Turn out dough onto a lightly floured work surface. Roll dough to an ⅛-inch thickness, and trim to a 14-inch square. Cut four 7-inch squares from dough. Brush entire surface of one square lightly with beaten egg white; place a filled apple in the center. Bring two adjacent corners of dough together at the tops, and press together to create a triangular flap (below left). Repeat, making four flaps (below right). Lightly brush one side of each flap with egg white, and press firmly against the apple. Repeat with remaining dough and apples. Transfer to a plate, and chill 15 minutes.

6. Mix together the egg yolk and heavy cream. Brush dumplings lightly with the egg wash, and transfer dumplings to a roasting pan, spacing dumplings at least 1 inch apart.

7. Bake 15 minutes. Reduce oven temperature to 375°. Remove roasting pan from oven, and pour the reserved syrup over dumplings. Return pan to the oven, and bake 10 minutes more, basting twice. Continue baking dumplings until deep-golden brown, about 10 minutes more. Transfer pan to a wire rack to cool slightly. Serve dumplings with the warm syrup.

34 *What a surprise whole-apple dumplings are after a brunch or light supper. A peeled McIntosh apple is stuffed with a spiced mixture of almonds and dried cherries, speared with a cinnamon stick, wrapped in pastry dough, and baked crisp. These three dumplings are served set in a warm syrup in a turn-of-the-century pressed-glass compote. Many other apples are excellent for baking and cooking, including Northern Spy, Cortland, Winesap, and Rome Beauty.*

35 *Quick puff pastry is used in this apple galette, a traditional French tart, which is caramelized on both the top and bottom. The apples are sliced very thin before being fanned around the top.*

35 caramelized-apple galette

*All-purpose flour, for
rolling out dough*

⅛ *pound Quick Puff Pastry
(recipe follows)*

1 *Northern Spy, or other firm
baking apple, peeled, cored,
and sliced in half lengthwise*

¼ *cup sugar*

2 *tablespoons unsalted butter*

2 *tablespoons Calvados or
brandy*

This tart bakes best in a cast-iron skillet. | **makes one 7½-inch-round galette**

1. Line a baking sheet with parchment. On a lightly floured work surface, roll out the puff-pastry dough to an ⅛-inch thickness. Using a paring knife, cut out a 7½-inch circle. Transfer the circle to prepared baking sheet, and chill 15 minutes.

2. Heat oven to 425°. Place the chilled dough in a cast-iron skillet that measures 6½ inches in diameter at the bottom. Using a mandoline or very sharp knife, slice the apple halves crosswise into twenty-five ⅛-inch-thick slices. Arrange the slices in a fan pattern, one overlapping another, keeping them ½ inch in from the edge of the dough; fill in the center with smaller or broken apple slices.

3. Sprinkle 2 tablespoons sugar over the apples, and dot with 1 tablespoon butter. Bake until pastry is golden brown and has puffed up along the edges, about 30 minutes.

4. Remove the skillet from the oven. Using a spatula, transfer the tart to a serving plate, and set aside.

5. Add remaining tablespoon butter to skillet, and set over medium heat. Add remaining 2 table-spoons sugar, and cook until sugar has dissolved and forms a light caramel, about 5 minutes. Pour Calvados into a glass, then pour into the skillet. Carefully ignite alcohol; allow flame to burn out.

6. Return tart to the skillet, apple-side down. Cook until the caramel bubbles up over the tart, and starts to look a little thick, 4 to 5 minutes. Remove from heat, and carefully invert the tart onto a serving plate, catching the hot caramel as it drips out of the skillet. Cut while warm, and serve.

quick puff pastry | makes 2 pounds

The dough for this quick pastry does not rise as much as the classic version does, but it tastes just as delicious. As you roll and fold the dough, it will become smoother and easier to handle with each turn; just make sure to roll out the dough to a half-inch thickness each time.

1¾ *cups all-purpose flour*

2 *cups cake flour (not self-rising)*

1 *teaspoon salt*

2 *cups (4 sticks) unsalted butter,
chilled and cut into pieces*

2 *tablespoons freshly squeezed
lemon juice*

1. In a large chilled bowl, sift together all-purpose flour, cake flour, and salt. Using a pastry knife, cut in the butter until only very small lumps, about ½ inch, remain.

2. In a small bowl, combine 1 cup ice water and the lemon juice. Stir into the flour mixture, a little at a time, pressing the dough together with your hands until it comes together. If necessary, add up to ¼ cup more ice water.

3. Turn dough out onto a well-floured work surface, and roll it into a 12-by-18-inch rectangle, about ½-inch thick; the dough will be very crumbly. Fold bottom of the rectangle toward the center, then fold the top over the bottom, like a letter. Give the dough a quarter turn to the right. Roll the dough into a large rectangle, ½ inch thick, and fold into thirds again.

4. Remove any excess flour with a dry, wide brush. Repeat rolling, folding, and turning process (step three) two more times. If the butter becomes too warm, transfer to refrigerator for a few minutes. Wrap the dough in plastic, and chill at least 1 hour.

5. Remove chilled dough from refrigerator. Repeat rolling, folding, and turning process again to execute one more double turn, for a total of six turns. Wrap dough in plastic, and store, refrigerated, up to 2 days or, frozen, up to 3 months.

36 acorn-squash and honey pie

3 small acorn squash
  (about 3 pounds)
1 teaspoon salt
½ teaspoon ground cinnamon
¾ teaspoon ground ginger
4 large whole eggs
½ cup plus 1 tablespoon milk
¾ cup honey
  All-purpose flour, for
  rolling out dough
  Cornmeal Pie Dough
1 large egg yolk
  Vegetable-oil cooking spray

An appealing alternative to pumpkin pie, these small pies are filled with acorn squash, a delicious yet underused vegetable. Here, it is sweetly, fragrantly flavored with honey, cinnamon, and ginger. Cornmeal gives the crust texture and enhances the pies' slightly nutty flavor. | **makes four 5-inch pies**

1. Cut the squash in half lengthwise, and remove all seeds. Steam until fork tender, 15 to 20 minutes. Set aside to cool. Coat four 5-inch pie pans lightly with cooking spray; set aside.

2. Scrape flesh from the shells of the cooled squash. Transfer flesh to bowl of a food processor, and purée until smooth. Add the salt, cinnamon, and ginger. Add the whole eggs, ½ cup milk, and honey. Pulse until thoroughly combined. Set the filling aside.

3. On a lightly floured surface, roll out one disk of pie dough to an ⅛-inch thickness. Drape the dough over the pie pan, trimming the edges to fit rim; create a decorative edge as desired. Repeat with the remaining dough and pie pans. Mix the egg yolk and remaining tablespoon milk; brush egg wash over the surface of the dough.

4. Heat oven to 425°. Divide filling among pie crusts. Bake 10 minutes. Lower oven temperature to 350°, and bake until custard has barely set, 25 to 30 minutes more; the custard will continue to cook as it cools. If crusts get too dark, make an aluminum-foil tent around crust. Transfer pies to wire racks to cool. Serve at room temperature or chilled. Store, refrigerated, up to 2 days.

cornmeal pie dough | **makes four 5-inch piecrusts**

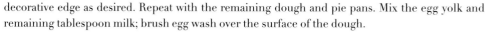

1½ cups all-purpose flour
½ cup yellow cornmeal,
  preferably stoneground
½ cup sugar
1 teaspoon salt
8 tablespoons (1 stick) unsalted
  butter, chilled and cut into
  small pieces
2 large egg yolks

In large bowl, mix together flour, cornmeal, sugar, and salt. Using your fingers, mix in butter until crumbly. In a small bowl, combine egg yolks and 3 tablespoons ice water. Add egg-yolk mixture to flour mixture. Using a fork, mix quickly and lightly. Knead dough lightly in bowl until dough holds together; add up to 1 tablespoon ice water if dry. Divide dough into four equal balls. Press each ball into a disk; wrap in plastic. Chill until firm, about 30 minutes.

37 deepest-dish apple pie

1 cup sugar

½ teaspoon ground cinnamon

1 teaspoon ground cardamom

6 tablespoons unsalted butter

15 Granny Smith apples (about 8
   pounds), peeled, cored, and cut
   into eighths

¾ teaspoon pure vanilla extract

6 tablespoons Calvados or
   brandy

½ cup plus 2 tablespoons
   heavy cream
   All-purpose flour, for
   rolling out dough

½ recipe Pâte Brisée (recipe,
   page 61)

1 large egg yolk
   Cheddar cheese, for garnish
   (optional)

You will need an ovenproof bowl to make this all-American deep-dish pie; we chose a 1930s stoneware casserole dish. Many bowls indicate on the bottom whether they are ovenproof. We decorated the top of the pie, before baking, with small, pearl-like balls of dough. | **makes one 8-inch pie**

1. In a small mixing bowl, combine the sugar, cinnamon, and cardamom. Set sugar mixture aside.

2. In a skillet, melt 2 tablespoons butter over medium-high heat. Add one-third of the apples, one-third of the sugar mixture, and ¼ teaspoon vanilla. Sauté until apples turn golden brown, about 4 minutes. Remove skillet from heat.

3. Measure 2 tablespoons Calvados into a cup, and add to skillet. Return skillet to heat, and cook 3 minutes. Calvados may ignite; proceed with caution until alcohol burns off, about 30 seconds. Add 3 tablespoons cream; cook, stirring, until thick, 2 to 3 minutes. Transfer cooked apples to a large bowl.

4. Repeat steps two and three two more times with the remaining apples.

5. On a lightly floured surface, roll out pâte brisée 3 inches larger than the ovenproof bowl (ours was eight inches wide and six inches deep), to an ⅛-inch thickness. Using a #4 plain pastry tip or ¼-inch tip, punch a hole in the center of the dough.

6. Place the apple mixture in ovenproof bowl; drape rolled-out pastry over the top, aligning hole over center of the dish. Trim overhanging edges to create a scalloped edge. Decorate top with any trimmings, using cold water to adhere.

7. In a small bowl, mix the egg yolk and the remaining tablespoon cream; brush mixture over dough. Chill 30 minutes.

8. Heat oven to 400°. Bake pie until golden brown, 50 to 55 minutes. Place a piece of aluminum foil over top to prevent further browning, and continue baking until pie bubbles. Transfer to a wire rack to cool, 1 hour. Serve with slices of cheddar cheese, if desired.

38 *A slice of chocolate-pecan pie with a chocolate crust is garnished with a spoonful of whipped cream. The tiny lavender blossoms sprinkled on top nicely complement both the dark pie and the nineteenth-century English purple transferware dessert plate.*

39 *One of Martha's favorite holiday desserts, this enchanting creation is assembled at the last minute simply by spooning chilled eggnog custard into a pastry shell that has been baked ahead of time in an oven-proof cup. We used a Victorian ironstone footed punch cup; it sits atop a nineteenth-century French porcelain plate. The "pie" is finished with a dollop of whipped cream.*

38 chocolate-pecan pie with chocolate crust

²⁄₃ cup sugar

1 cup light corn syrup

4 ounces semisweet chocolate, chopped into ½-inch chunks

2 tablespoons unsalted butter
All-purpose flour, for rolling out dough
Chocolate-Crust Dough (recipe follows)

3 large eggs

1 teaspoon pure vanilla extract

1½ cups pecan halves

2 tablespoons fresh or dried lavender, for garnish

1 cup whipped cream or crème fraîche
Vegetable-oil cooking spray

Like all pecan pies, this one uses a mixture of sugar and corn syrup to achieve its distinctive texture. The chocolate crust is a delicious way to underscore the chocolate in the filling. | **makes one 9-inch pie**

1. In a medium saucepan, combine sugar and corn syrup. Set over medium-high heat, and stir to partially dissolve sugar. Bring to boil, and reduce heat to low. Simmer 2 minutes, stirring occasionally. Cool completely, 45 minutes. Set aside to thicken.

2. In a heat-proof bowl or the top of double boiler, combine 2 ounces chocolate and butter; set over a pan of simmering water. Cook until melted. Set aside to cool.

3. Heat oven to 400°. On lightly floured surface, roll out the chocolate-crust dough to a 13-inch circle, about ⅛ inch thick. Coat a 9-inch pie pan with cooking spray. Place dough in the pan, and crimp the edges. Chill 15 minutes.

4. In large bowl, beat eggs until foamy. Add reserved chocolate and corn-syrup mixtures. Stir in the vanilla and pecan halves; set filling aside.

5. Pour filling into the crust. Bake 20 minutes. Lower oven temperature to 350°, and bake until filling has set, about 20 minutes. Sprinkle with remaining 2 ounces chocolate, and bake 5 minutes more. Transfer to a wire rack to cool, 1¼ hours. Serve with whipped cream; garnish with lavender, if desired.

chocolate-crust dough | **makes one 9-inch piecrust**

1¼ cups all-purpose flour

2 tablespoons unsweetened cocoa powder

6 tablespoons unsalted butter, chilled

3 large egg yolks

⅓ cup sugar

½ teaspoon salt

½ teaspoon pure vanilla extract

In a large bowl, sift together the flour and cocoa powder. In small bowl, using a fork, combine the remaining ingredients; add to cocoa mixture. Using your fingers, combine until mixture holds together and no large lumps of butter remain. Turn mixture out onto clean work surface; knead until smooth, about 1 minute. Flatten into a disk, and wrap in plastic. Chill at least 30 minutes.

39 eggnog cups

7 large egg yolks

⅔ cup sugar

2 tablespoons all-purpose
   flour, sifted

2 cups milk

½ vanilla bean, split lengthwise

1 teaspoon freshly grated nutmeg
   All-purpose flour, for
   rolling out dough
   Pâte Brisée (recipe, page 61)

1 tablespoon plus 1 cup
   heavy cream

2 tablespoons confectioners'
   sugar, sifted

1 tablespoon rum

The range of tones in this dessert's golden crust looks especially pretty draped around a plain white cup. If you're not sure that your cups are ovenproof, use six-ounce ramekins. | **makes 8**

1. Combine 6 egg yolks and the sugar in the bowl of an electric mixer fitted with whisk attachment. Mix on high speed until mixture is thick and pale yellow, and holds a ribbonlike trail on the surface for a few seconds when you raise the whisk, about 5 minutes. Add flour; mix until fully incorporated.

2. Combine milk, vanilla, and nutmeg in a 2-quart stainless-steel saucepan; bring mixture to a boil over medium-high heat. With mixer running, pour about one-fourth of milk mixture into egg mixture. Slowly add this new mixture to the saucepan with the remaining milk. Cook over medium heat, whisking constantly, until mixture thickens and bubbles in center, 4 to 5 minutes. Pass through a sieve into a medium bowl. Place plastic wrap directly on surface to prevent a skin from forming. Let cool, 30 to 45 minutes. Chill custard until set, at least 2 hours.

3. On a lightly floured surface, roll out pâte brisée to an ⅛-inch thickness. Cut into eight 6-inch squares. Place each square in an ovenproof cup, allowing excess to drape 1 to 1½ inches over edges.

4. In a small bowl, mix the remaining egg yolk and 1 tablespoon cream; brush over surface of dough. Chill at least 1 hour.

5. Heat oven to 350°. Place cups on a baking sheet, and gently prick the bottom of dough three to four times with a fork. Bake until crust turns a deep golden color and inside of pastry shell is dry, 20 to 25 minutes. Transfer to a wire rack to cool completely.

6. Chill the bowl and whisk attachment of an electric mixer. Whip the remaining cup cream on medium-high speed. When cream starts to thicken, add confectioners' sugar, and mix until soft peaks form. Add rum, and continue to whip until soft peaks return. Spoon ¼ cup chilled custard into each shell. Add a dollop of the whipped cream, and serve.

40 raisin pie

1½ cups golden raisins
1½ cups dark raisins
 1 cup sugar
¼ cup all-purpose flour, plus
    more for rolling out dough
 2 tablespoons freshly squeezed
    lemon juice, plus zest of 1 lemon
    Pâte Brisée (recipe, page 61)
 1 egg yolk
 1 tablespoon heavy cream
    Vegetable-oil cooking spray

You can make the holes in the top layer of dough with a pastry tip, available at specialty baking-supply stores, or with a straw. | **makes one 9-inch pie**

1. Combine all raisins in a large bowl, and cover with boiling water. Let soak 15 minutes. Drain in a colander, and return raisins to bowl. Add sugar, flour, lemon juice, and lemon zest. Mix thoroughly, and set mixture aside to thicken, about 10 minutes. Coat a 9-inch metal pie pan lightly with cooking spray, and set pan aside.

2. On a lightly floured work surface, roll out half of the pâte brisée to an ⅛-inch thickness, and drape over a 9-inch pie pan. Trim so dough fits to the lip of the pan, with no overhang.

3. Roll out remaining half of pâte brisée to an ⅛-inch thickness. Using a ruler, measure a 9-inch circle in center, marking lightly without cutting through dough. Using a #4 pastry tip or a straw, punch 10 to 12 rows of holes in the dough. Work quickly, so dough remains cold and holes form easily.

4. Fill the prepared pie pan with the reserved raisin mixture. Using a pastry brush, gently brush the edges with cool water. Top with the perforated circle of dough, making sure it is centered. Using scissors, trim excess dough so that it creates an overhang of ½ inch. Tuck in the overhanging dough so it just sits on top of rim. Chill 30 minutes.

5. Heat oven to 425°. Mix egg yolk and cream in a small bowl. Brush pie sparingly with the egg wash.

6. Place pie on a baking sheet, and transfer to oven. Bake 20 minutes, and reduce oven temperature to 375°. Bake 35 to 40 minutes more. If pie starts to get too brown, drape a piece of aluminum foil over top. Transfer to a wire rack to cool.

40 *A honeycomb top crust adds an unusual touch to this traditional Pennsylvania-Dutch raisin pie. The filling, a simple mixture of raisins, sugar, lemon, eggs, and heavy cream, thickens for just a few minutes before it is spooned into the crust for baking. A slice is served here on a late-nineteenth-century floral sheet-transfer dessert plate.*

41 *This not-quite-traditional trifle is a wonderful way to serve fresh figs and the summer's best berries — we used red and golden raspberries, blackberries, and strawberries. Toasted génoise and a tart, creamy lemon curd set off the fruit, which has been briefly marinated in sugar and Grand Marnier. An amber Depression-glass plate makes it all even more dazzling.*

chapter four

Fruit Desserts

Take advantage of
every season's colorful gifts,
each in its turn, each at
its pinnacle of flavor

Fruit—ripe and unadorned—is the original dessert. A dense fig, a crisp apple, the reddest June strawberries—what more do you need? Well, perhaps a way to cradle them. Of course, you could bake a pie or an upside-down cake, always wonderful choices. But there is another world of fruit desserts, where the texture, color, or sweetness of fresh fruit is lifted like a jewel in its setting. The desserts that follow range from the very simple, like blood oranges soaked in honey and lemon, to the fantastic, like our berry vacherin, a stack of meringues, whipped cream, and summer berries. ❋ With so many splendid growers and distributors around the world, countless varieties of fruit are available all year long. But the best is always had at the peak of season. Whether you're shopping at a farm stand or a grocery store, use your eyes and your nose. If fruit looks ripe, smell it. If there is no scent, it isn't ripe, and it may never be. Hard, autumn fruits like pears and apples should be firm to the touch, never bruised or mushy. Berries should be deeply colored from end to end. Always remove them from their container so those on top won't crush those below; spread them on a baking sheet lined with paper towel, and discard any that are damaged, moldy, or unripe. Keep them, loosely covered with paper towel or plastic wrap, in the refrigerator. Blueberries will last up to a week, but raspberries and strawberries should be eaten within a few days. Rinse them before using. ❋ Trust your taste, but also trust nature, because what you had in mind may not always be what's in season. One berry can nearly always take the place of another, just as apples can usually substitute for pears. By starting with the choicest ingredients, you can create endlessly inspired variations on nature's sweetest theme.

41 fig-and-berry trifle

1 pint (about 18) green or black figs, stemmed and quartered

1 pint mixed berries, larger fruit hulled and quartered

¼ cup granulated sugar

1 tablespoon Grand Marnier Yellow Génoise Cake (recipe follows) Lemon-Curd and Whipped-Cream Filling (recipe follows) Confectioners' sugar, for dusting

Just a few minutes of last-minute assembly are needed to serve this summery dessert; the cake and lemon curd can be made several days in advance. | **serves 6**

1. Combine the figs and mixed berries in a small bowl. Sprinkle with granulated sugar, and drizzle Grand Marnier over top. Let macerate, tossing gently once or twice, until juicy, about 30 minutes.

2. Heat oven to 425°. Slice génoise into twelve 3-inch squares; use any extras for snacking. Place squares on a baking pan, and toast until golden brown, 6 to 8 minutes. Transfer to a wire rack to cool.

3. Place a square on each of six serving plates. Spoon lemon curd and macerated fruit over the squares. Top with another génoise square, dust with the confectioners' sugar, and serve.

yellow génoise cake | **makes one 11½-by-17½-inch sheet cake**

6 tablespoons unsalted butter, melted, plus more for pan

1⅓ cups all-purpose flour, plus more for pan

1 cup sugar

6 large eggs

1 teaspoon pure vanilla extract

Génoise, or French sponge cake, differs from regular sponge cake because it uses butter, which makes it more tender and flavorful. It can be refrigerated up to three days or frozen up to one month.

1. Heat oven to 350°. Butter an 11½-by-17½-inch jelly-roll pan, and line with parchment paper. Butter and flour the paper, and set prepared pan aside.

2. Set the heat-proof bowl of an electric mixer over, but not touching, a pan of simmering water. Combine the sugar and eggs in bowl, and whisk until mixture is warm to the touch, about 2 minutes.

3. Return bowl to electric mixer, and beat on high speed until mixture is very thick and pale, 6 to 8 minutes. With a rubber spatula, gently transfer mixture to a large mixing bowl. Working in three additions, sift in flour, folding gently after each. In a small bowl, combine the butter and the vanilla; then add butter mixture in a steady stream as you fold in the third flour addition. Fold gently, and pour onto prepared pan. Smooth top with an offset spatula.

4. Bake until cake is springy to the touch and golden brown, 18 to 20 minutes. Let cool on a wire rack.

5. When ready to use, turn out cake onto a cutting board covered with a piece of parchment paper, and peel the parchment from the bottom of the cake.

lemon-curd and whipped-cream filling | **makes 2¾ cups**

6 large egg yolks

1 cup granulated sugar

½ cup freshly squeezed lemon juice (about 3 lemons), strained, plus grated zest of 1 lemon

8 tablespoons (1 stick) unsalted butter, cut into small pieces

⅔ cup heavy cream

1 tablespoon confectioners' sugar

The lemon-curd base for this filling can be made several days before it's needed, but it should be prepared at least a few hours in advance so it can chill. Fold in the whipped cream on the day you need the filling.

1. In a small, heavy, stainless-steel saucepan, whisk together egg yolks, granulated sugar, and lemon juice. Set pan over medium heat, and cook, stirring constantly with a wooden spoon, until thick enough to coat back the back of the spoon, 6 to 10 minutes.

2. Transfer mixture to a small bowl. Stir in the butter, piece by piece. Add the zest, and let cool completely. Lay a piece of plastic wrap directly on the surface to prevent a skin from forming, and chill.

3. Combine heavy cream and confectioners' sugar in a chilled metal bowl. Whip until stiff peaks form. Fold whipped-cream mixture into lemon curd, and chill at least 20 minutes.

42 *Strawberries have surely never tasted this intense. Before they are added to this napoleon, they are roasted with vanilla, which softens them and draws out their inherent sweetness. The napoleon begins with a layer of puff pastry topped with neatly piped orange pastry cream and those juicy strawberries, then gets another layer of puff pastry spread with sweetened whipped cream and a sprinkling of chopped pistachios. The open-handled tray is French porcelain.*

43 *These lighter-than-air shells of crisp meringue hold little pillows of tart crème fraîche topped with pitted fresh red cherries. Three little bites on a rippled-edge milk-glass plate decorated with a cherry leaf make a playful yet elegant dessert—perfect for an afternoon wedding or a graduation party. You'll need a pastry bag to pipe the meringue and just a paper clip to pit the cherries.*

42 roasted-strawberry napoleon

2 tablespoons light corn syrup

1 sheet frozen puff pastry,
   from standard package
   (17 ¼ ounces), thawed

2 tablespoons unsalted butter,
   room temperature

½ vanilla bean, split in
   half lengthwise

14 medium strawberries (about
   one pint), stems trimmed

1 tablespoon granulated sugar

2 tablespoons Grand Marnier
   (optional)

1 tablespoon freshly squeezed
   orange juice

½ cup heavy cream

1 tablespoon confectioners' sugar
   Orange Pastry Cream
   (recipe follows)

1 tablespoon finely chopped
   pistachios

If you don't make your own puff pastry, buy some from a local bakery or use the best-quality frozen kind you can find. You will find vanilla beans at specialty food stores or through specialty-food catalogs. | **serves 4**

1. Heat oven to 375°. Line a baking pan with parchment paper, and set aside. Have ready another baking pan, unlined. In a small bowl, combine the corn syrup with 1 teaspoon warm water; set aside.

2. Lightly dust a clean work surface with flour. Roll puff-pastry into a 12-inch square; trim edges. Cut sheet on fold lines, making three 4-by-12-inch rectangles. Place rectangles on lined pan. Top with another piece of parchment. Place the unlined pan on top of the filled pan. Bake 8 minutes.

3. Remove the empty pan and top parchment from the pan, and return to oven. Bake until pastry starts to puff and is light-golden brown, about 8 minutes. Remove from oven; lightly brush with reserved corn-syrup mixture. Using a long metal spatula, gently flip rectangles. Brush again with corn-syrup mixture. Bake until shiny and golden brown, about 9 minutes more. With the spatula, transfer puff pastry to a wire rack to cool completely. Store in an airtight container until ready to use.

4. Increase oven temperature to 450°. Using a pastry brush, coat the bottom of a medium oven-proof sauté pan with 1 tablespoon butter; scrape vanilla seeds into butter. Place strawberries, cut sides down, in pan. Sprinkle with granulated sugar, and lay vanilla pod on top. Roast until strawberries start to "slump" and feel soft when squeezed, 10 to 12 minutes. Using a slotted spoon, transfer all but two of the berries and vanilla pod to a plate to cool. Reserve juices in pan.

5. Set pan over high heat. If using Grand Marnier, add to pan, and light a match, carefully igniting alcohol; allow flame to burn out, about 1 minute. Reduce heat to medium. Using a fork, mash two remaining strawberries, and add orange juice. (If not using Grand Marnier, add 2 tablespoons more orange juice.) Cook until thick and syrupy, 30 to 40 seconds; discard vanilla pod. Remove from heat. Swirl in the remaining tablespoon butter, and set aside.

6. Combine cream and confectioners' sugar in bowl of an electric mixer; whip until stiff peaks form.

7. Without using a tip, close off the end of a pastry bag with a paper clip or clothespin; fill with whipped cream. Repeat, filling a second pastry bag with orange pastry cream. (Alternatively, use two resealable plastic bags, and cut off a corner on each; an offset spatula can also be used to spread both whipped and pastry creams.)

8. Pipe a tablespoon of pastry cream in the middle of a serving plate. Center a rectangle of puff pastry on top. Leaving a ½-inch border, pipe orange pastry cream onto puff pastry. Arrange the roasted strawberries on top of pastry cream; scrape any remaining juices from plate into reserved sauce. Place a second rectangle of puff pastry on top of strawberries. Leaving a ½-inch border, pipe whipped cream onto second rectangle of puff pastry. Sprinkle with pistachios. Place a third rectangle of puff pastry on top.

9. Using a serrated knife, slice napoleon into four pieces. Drizzle with the reserved sauce, and serve.

orange pastry cream | **makes 1 cup**

1 *cup milk*

2 *one-by-two-inch strips orange*
zest (1 orange)

¼ *cup sugar*

½ *vanilla bean, split lengthwise*

2 *tablespoons cornstarch*

1 *large whole egg*

1 *large egg yolk*

2 *tablespoons unsalted butter,*
cut into small pieces

1. In a small saucepan, combine milk, orange zest, and 2 tablespoons sugar. Scrape in the vanilla seeds, and add the pod. Bring the mixture to a boil over medium-high heat, stirring occasionally. Remove from heat, and cover. Set aside 10 minutes; discard the orange zest and vanilla pod.

2. Have ready an ice-water bath. In a small bowl, mix together the remaining 2 tablespoons sugar with the cornstarch. In a medium bowl, whisk together the egg and egg yolk; add the sugar mixture, and continue whisking until pale yellow.

3. Return milk mixture to a boil, scraping vanilla seeds from sides of pan.

4. Slowly ladle half of boiling milk mixture into egg-yolk mixture, whisking constantly. Transfer this new mixture back to saucepan.

5. Set pan over medium heat, whisking constantly and scraping sides and edges of pan. Once mixture comes to a boil, whisk vigorously until very thick, about 1½ minutes.

6. Remove pan from heat. Using a rubber spatula, scrape pastry cream into a medium bowl; set over ice-water bath. Whisk butter, piece by piece, into the pastry cream while still warm. Let cool completely. Lay plastic wrap on surface of pastry cream to prevent a skin from forming; wrap tightly. Store pastry cream, refrigerated, up to 1 day.

43 cherry-meringue bites

4 *large egg whites*

1 *cup granulated sugar*
Pinch cream of tartar

¾ *cup crème fraîche*

50 *cherries (about 1 pound), pitted*
Confectioners' sugar,
for dusting

These meringue cups can be made several days in advance and stored in an airtight container. When you're ready to assemble the desserts, begin at step five. If you want to pit the cherries and leave the stems intact, unfold a paper clip at its center, and, depending on the size of the cherry, insert either the large or small end of the paper clip through the bottom of the fruit, loosen pit, and pull out. | **makes 50**

1. Cut two pieces of parchment paper to fit two baking sheets. Using a 1-inch cookie cutter, draw twenty-five circles on each piece of parchment. Turn the paper over, and place on sheets. Set aside.

2. Combine the egg whites, granulated sugar, and cream of tartar in the heat-proof bowl of an electric mixer. Set the bowl over a pan of simmering water. Whisk constantly until the sugar has dissolved and the whites are warm to the touch, 2 to 3 minutes.

3. Heat oven to 200°. Transfer the bowl to the electric mixer. Starting on low speed and gradually increasing to high, whip until stiff, glossy peaks form, 10 to 12 minutes.

4. Fit a pastry bag with a Wilton #16 star tip, and fill bag with the meringue. Cover one of the circles with an even layer of meringue. Pipe around the circumference, making a 1-inch-high cup. Repeat piping over the remaining circles. Transfer baking sheets to oven, and bake 20 minutes. Reduce the heat to 175°, and bake until the meringue has dried but is still white, 35 to 40 minutes more. Transfer baking sheets to a wire rack, and let cool completely.

5. Fit a pastry bag with a plain round tip, and fill bag with crème fraîche. Pipe 1½ teaspoons crème fraîche into each meringue cup; top with a cherry. Dust with confectioners' sugar, and serve.

44 caramelized-apple crepes

½ cup all-purpose flour
Pinch of salt
2 large eggs
1 egg yolk
1¼ cups milk
1½ teaspoons pure vanilla extract
6 tablespoons unsalted butter
6 crisp apples, such as Mutsu,
 peeled, quartered, and cut
 into 1-inch chunks
2 tablespoons lemon juice plus 1
 tablespoon lemon zest (1 lemon)
½ teaspoon cinnamon
½ teaspoon ground ginger
6 tablespoons granulated sugar
3 tablespoons Calvados or
 brandy
1 cup crème fraîche
3 tablespoons confectioners'
 sugar, plus more for dusting

Be sure to choose crisp apples whose texture will stand up nicely as they are cooked. We used Mutsu, but Granny Smith also work well. | **serves 6**

1. In a medium bowl, sift together flour and salt. Whisk in eggs, egg yolk, and about 1 tablespoon milk, forming a smooth batter with a pastelike consistency. Add remaining milk and 1 teaspoon vanilla; mix until no lumps remain. Melt 4 tablespoons butter in a nonstick skillet, and stir into the batter; leave a film of butter in the skillet. Let the batter rest at room temperature about 30 minutes.

2. Heat oven to warm. Over medium-low heat, warm the skillet thoroughly. Stir batter, and carefully ladle about ¼ cup batter into skillet. Rotate skillet so batter spreads out and thinly coats the bottom and edges of the skillet. Return skillet to heat, and cook crepe until edges turn golden brown, lacy, and start to pull away from the skillet, about 2 minutes. Using a knife or an offset spatula, carefully turn crepe over; cook other side until just golden, about 30 to 40 seconds. Slide the crepe onto a heat-proof plate. Repeat with the remaining batter, stirring it before making another crepe. Stack cooked crepes on top of one another.

3. Loosely cover plate of crepes with aluminum foil, and place in the oven to keep warm.

4. Place apples in a medium bowl. Add lemon juice, lemon zest, cinnamon, and ginger. Toss to coat.

5. Melt the remaining 2 tablespoons butter in a 12-inch cast-iron skillet set over medium heat. Add granulated sugar, and cook, stirring occasionally, until sugar turns amber in color, about 5 minutes. If caramel starts to get too dark, remove skillet from heat. Add apples, and cook, turning apples over, until soft and completely caramelized. Pour Calvados into a measuring cup, then pour into skillet. Carefully ignite the alcohol, and allow the flame to burn out, 2 to 3 minutes, shaking skillet to toss the apples in the syrup. Remove apples from heat; let cool slightly.

6. Combine the crème fraîche, remaining ½ teaspoon vanilla, and confectioners' sugar in a chilled mixing bowl. Whip mixture until light, fluffy, and almost doubled in volume.

7. Remove crepes from oven, and transfer to six serving plates. Spoon a scant ½ cup caramelized apples onto each crepe, and dust lightly with confectioners' sugar. Spoon a generous amount of crème-fraîche mixture over apples. Fold crepes, and serve immediately.

44 Apples arrive in the market just as appetites turn from bright summer tastes to warmly spiced fall flavors. These chunks of Mutsu apples are caramelized in sugar, flavored with lemon zest and spices, flamed with brandy, and wrapped in warm crepes with crème fraîche and a dusting of confectioners' sugar.

45 *Fresh green figs,
poached in Sauternes and flavored
with spices, including a cinnamon
stick and star anise, are exquisite
in this classic, creamy white
Wedgwood bowl. The figs are
served halved, floating in the sauce;
if you like, add a dollop of our
vanilla mascarpone on the side.
You can use the same poaching
liquid for other fruit: Try pears,
which have a strong enough
texture to stand up to cooking.*

45 spiced poached figs

2 cups sweet white wine,
  such as Sauternes
¾ cup sugar
2 two-inch strips fresh lemon peel
8 whole black peppercorns
1 two-inch-long stick cinnamon
2 bay leaves
2 sprigs fresh thyme
2 thin slices fresh ginger
2 whole star anise
3 green cardamom pods
8 large whole green or purple figs
½ cup mascarpone cheese
1½ tablespoons confectioners'
  sugar, sifted
½ vanilla bean

These figs can be made the day before you need them and refrigerated; bring them to room temperature before serving. Choose fresh figs that are not overly ripe; otherwise they may fall apart while poaching. | **serves 4**

1. Combine the wine, sugar, lemon peel, peppercorns, cinnamon stick, bay leaves, thyme, ginger, star anise, and cardamom in a small, deep saucepan. Place pan over medium-high heat, and bring to a boil. Reduce heat to low, and simmer 10 minutes. Cover, and simmer 20 minutes more.

2. Add the figs to the syrup. Return syrup to a simmer, and cover. Poach gently until the figs are soft but not mushy, 10 to 15 minutes. Transfer figs and syrup to a bowl, and let stand until cool and steam no longer rises. Cover with plastic, and refrigerate overnight.

3. Combine the mascarpone and confectioners' sugar in a medium bowl. Split the vanilla bean lengthwise. Using a paring knife, scrape the seeds into the bowl with the mascarpone mixture; reserve pod for another use. Using a spoon or rubber spatula, stir until well combined.

4. Remove chilled figs and syrup from refrigerator, and let stand until room temperature. Transfer figs to another bowl, and strain syrup; reserve solids for garnish.

5. Place two figs, sliced in half, in the center of each plate. Spoon some poaching liquid over plate, and place a dollop of vanilla mascarpone next to figs. Garnish with reserved solids, if desired.

46 blood oranges with honey

8 blood oranges
¼ cup honey
  Freshly squeezed juice
  of 2 lemons
  Mint sprigs, for garnish

We like to bring soaked blood oranges, with their surprising red flesh and extra-sweet flavor, to the table in a blown-glass trifle dish. Usually seedless, these oranges have hints of strawberry and raspberry, and are less acidic than other varieties. Look for them during the winter and early spring; choose firm, heavy, thin-skinned fruit with a smooth, fine texture. | **serves 8**

1. Working over a bowl, remove pith and peel from the oranges with a knife; reserve any juice.

2. In a large saucepan, combine the honey, lemon juice, and 4 cups water. Bring liquid to a simmer, and remove from heat. Add the oranges and reserved juice. Let stand until cool, and transfer to the refrigerator.

3. When ready to serve, garnish with mint sprigs.

47 *Lifted on a footed iron-stone platter, clouds of meringue and whipped cream make a glorious setting for fraises des bois, the very small wild strawberries, as well as raspberries and fresh red currants. This vacherin, so called because its shape resembles the French cheese of the same name, would be a wonderful summer substitute for a birthday cake, perhaps for someone who doesn't care to blow out candles.*

48 *In this luscious, sophisticated version of the classic peach melba, a sabayon made from eggs, sparkling white wine, and heavy cream replaces the traditional vanilla ice cream. The flavor of the peaches is drawn out by sautéing them with butter and sugar until they have caramelized. On top is a warm raspberry sauce. A hand-blown port glass shows off the three lovely layers.*

47 berry vacherin

6 large egg whites, room
  temperature
1½ cups granulated sugar
2 teaspoons pure vanilla extract
1½ cups heavy cream
2 tablespoons confectioners'
  sugar, plus more for dusting
1½ pints mixed berries, such as red
  and white fraises des bois,
  red and golden raspberries,
  and fresh red currants
  Red-Raspberry Sauce
  (recipe follows)

The crisp meringue shells are difficult to cut without creating crumbles, but you can lessen breakage by using a very thin, sharp knife. | **serves 10**

1. Heat oven to 200°. Cut two pieces of parchment paper to line two baking sheets. On each piece of parchment, trace a 9-inch circle. Place parchment, pencil sides down, on baking sheets. Set aside.

2. Place the egg whites in the bowl of an electric mixer. Beat on high speed until soft peaks form, about 2 minutes. Add ¼ cup granulated sugar; beat to combine. Gradually add the remaining 1¼ cups granulated sugar, 1 tablespoon at a time, until the whites are very stiff and glossy. Add 1 teaspoon vanilla; beat just until combined.

3. Divide batter between the traced circles. Using an icing or rubber spatula, spread batter in an even layer to edges of circles.

4. Bake meringue disks about 3½ hours, rotating sheets between racks every 30 minutes. The disks should be white, dried, and crisp on the outside, yet soft and somewhat chewy inside; test by tapping the center lightly with a fork. Transfer baking sheets to wire racks; let disks cool completely.

5. Combine cream, the remaining teaspoon vanilla, and confectioners' sugar in a chilled metal bowl; whip until cream is stiff but soft.

6. Place one meringue disk on a serving plate. Spread three-fourths of the whipped cream over disk. Sprinkle with half of the berries, and top with the second meringue disk. Spoon remaining cream onto center of disk, and heap remaining berries on top. Dust with confectioners' sugar. Serve immediately with the red-raspberry sauce on the side.

red-raspberry sauce | **makes about ¾ cup**

This easy-to-make berry sauce can also be used over ice cream or sliced peaches.

1 pint raspberries
¼ cup sugar
2 tablespoons freshly squeezed
  lemon juice
  Pinch of salt

Combine all ingredients in a small, nonreactive saucepan set over low heat. Cook until berries release their juices and just start to break down, about 5 minutes. Using a rubber spatula, press berries through a fine sieve; discard solids. Let cool. Store, refrigerated, in an airtight container.

48 caramelized-peach melba

3 *large ripe peaches*
  (about 1¼ pounds)
2 *tablespoons unsalted butter*
½ *cup sugar*
4 *large egg yolks*
½ *cup Moscato d'Asti (sweet,*
  sparkling white wine) or
  champagne
½ *cup heavy cream*
  Warm Raspberry Sauce
  (recipe follows)

The sabayon for this dessert can be made up to twenty-four hours ahead and stored, refrigerated, in an airtight container. Fold in the whipped cream just before serving. | **serves 6**

1. Bring a large saucepan of water to a boil, and have ready an ice-water bath. Cut an "x" in the bottom of the peaches, and place them in the boiling water. Blanch until skins loosen, 1 to 2 minutes. Using a slotted spoon, transfer peaches to ice-water bath to stop cooking process. Peel the peaches, and cut in half; discard pits.

2. Melt butter in a skillet set over medium-high heat. Sprinkle ¼ cup sugar over butter. Add the peaches, cut sides down. Cook until peaches start to brown, about 4 minutes. Reduce heat to medium; cook until sugar caramelizes, about 6 minutes more, spooning syrup over the peaches occasionally. Reduce heat to low; turn peaches over, and cook until the caramel turns amber in color, about 2 minutes more. Remove pan from heat, and let cool.

3. Combine remaining ¼ cup sugar and egg yolks in heat-proof bowl of an electric mixer fitted with paddle attachment; beat until pale and thick, about 2 minutes, scraping down sides of bowl once. Add Moscato; beat 2 minutes more. Set over a pan of briskly simmering water. Whisk until sabayon thickens, is fluffy, and is slightly stiff, about 3 minutes. Transfer bowl to the ice-water bath. Continue whisking sabayon until chilled, at least 3 minutes.

4. In a large chilled bowl, whip the cream until medium-stiff peaks form; fold into the chilled sabayon.

5. To serve, divide mixture among six goblets. Top with peach halves and 3 tablespoons sauce.

warm raspberry sauce | makes 1¼ cups

2 *cups raspberries*
¼ *cup sugar*
1 *tablespoon freshly squeezed*
  lemon juice

Combine all ingredients and 2 tablespoons water in a small saucepan set over medium-low heat. Cook until berries release some of their juices but remain whole, about 5 minutes. Let cool slightly.

49 pears and pecorino

½ *pound pecorino cheese*
4 *Comice pears, cored and sliced*
  Honey, for drizzling
  Freshly ground pepper

Few desserts are as naturally sophisticated as fruit paired with cheese, especially when served on a pretty plate, like this pink-and-gilt-bordered porcelain one. Pecorino, a hard, aged Italian cheese made from sheep's milk, works especially well with ripe, juicy Comice pears. If you can't find pecorino, substitute another hard cheese, like Parmesan. The honey and ground pepper complete the marvelous quartet of sweet and pungent flavors. | **serves 4**

Slice cheese thinly, and divide among four plates. Place pears on top of cheese. Warm the honey, and drizzle it over plates. Top with a grind of pepper.

50 summer-berry molds

7½ cups mixed blackberries and
    raspberries, plus 1 cup to
    garnish
½   cup sugar
¾   cup ruby port
1½ teaspoons powdered
    unflavored gelatin
12 Meringue Disks (recipe follows)

We used both blackberries and raspberries for these little gelatin molds, but you can use any fresh summer berries you can find. | serves 6

1. Combine 6¼ cups berries and 6 tablespoons sugar in a medium bowl. Pour port over berries. Smash berries lightly with a fork, and let stand at room temperature 1 hour.

2. Pour mixture into a sieve set over a bowl, and let drain 30 minutes. Set solids aside; pass juice through a cheesecloth-lined sieve into a bowl.

3. Pour ½ cup berry juice into a heat-proof bowl or the top of a double boiler. Sprinkle gelatin over top; let stand until softened, about 5 minutes. Set bowl over a pan of simmering water; whisk mixture until the gelatin dissolves, about 5 minutes. Remove bowl from heat; add the remaining berry juice.

4. Divide 1¼ cups berries among six 6-ounce ramekins. Pour gelatin mixture over berries. Cover with plastic, and refrigerate until set, about 4 hours.

5. Combine reserved berry solids, remaining 2 tablespoons sugar, and ¼ cup water in a saucepan. Set over medium heat; cook, stirring occasionally, 5 minutes. Press sauce through a sieve set over a bowl.

6. To serve, place a meringue disk on a plate. Unmold gelatin by dipping ramekin briefly into a hot-water bath and running a knife tip around the edge; invert gelatin onto disk; top with another disk. Repeat with remaining disks and gelatin. Garnish with remaining whole berries and the berry sauce.

meringue disks | makes 16

    Unsalted butter, melted,
    for pans
    All-purpose flour, for pans
5½ tablespoons plus ½ cup sugar
½   cup whole blanched almonds
4   large egg whites
¼   teaspoon cream of tartar
1   tablespoon plus 1 teaspoon
    cornstarch, sifted
½   teaspoon distilled white vinegar

1. Cut two pieces of parchment paper to line two baking sheets. On each piece of parchment, trace eight 3¼-inch circles. Place parchment, pencil sides down, on baking sheets. Lightly brush parchment with butter; dust with flour. Tap off any excess.

2. Combine 5½ tablespoons sugar and almonds in the bowl of a food processor; pulse until a fine powder forms. Set almond mixture aside.

3. Heat oven to 225°. In the bowl of an electric mixer fitted with the paddle attachment, beat egg whites and cream of tartar on medium speed until foamy, about 5 minutes. Increase speed to medium high; slowly add remaining ½ cup sugar. Beat until glossy and firm, 5 minutes. Reduce speed to low; sprinkle cornstarch over top, and mix 15 to 20 seconds. Add vinegar; mix 15 to 20 seconds more.

4. Fold in the reserved almond mixture with a rubber spatula. Place ¼ cup batter in center of each circle; using an icing or rubber spatula, spread batter in an even layer to edges of circles.

5. Bake 1 hour 15 minutes, rotating pans between shelves halfway through cooking time. Transfer parchment with meringue disks to wire racks to cool. Store in an airtight container until ready to use.

50 *A white plate shows off a colorful dessert: an individual serving of berry gelatin sandwiched between two light meringues. The gelatin, molded in a ramekin, is enhanced with ruby port and a few plump berries. The plate is garnished with a few more berries, berry sauce, and a sprig of mint.*

52, 53 & 54

Our versions of some milk-and-cookies classics — chocolate-chunk, oatmeal-pecan chocolate-chunk, and ginger cookies — are all somewhat larger than usual, which we think makes them even more satisfying. They all freeze well, or can be stored at room temperature in an airtight container for several days. The octagonal platter is nineteenth-century ironstone.

55 *Tender and crumbly shortbread, long associated with Christmas, is an alliance among four simple ingredients: butter, flour, sugar, and salt. A cookie that has no rival in the purity of its taste, shortbread descended from the Scottish bannock, which was made with oat and barley meal. Shortbread is now made with wheat flour. Baked in rounds and cut into wedges, it recalls the ancient New Year cakes that symbolized the sun.*

52 living large chocolate-chunk cookies

1 cup (2 sticks) unsalted butter,
  room temperature
½ teaspoon salt
1 teaspoon pure vanilla extract
¾ cup packed dark-brown sugar
½ cup granulated sugar
1 large egg
½ teaspoon baking soda
2 cups sifted all-purpose flour
1 cup chocolate chunks or
  chopped bittersweet chocolate

Buy chocolate that's already been chunked, or cut up your favorite chocolate bar. | **makes about 1 dozen**

1. In the bowl of an electric mixer fitted with the paddle attachment, beat butter, salt, and vanilla until fluffy. Add both sugars; beat until lightened in color, 4 minutes. Beat in the egg.

2. Add the baking soda and flour; beat on low speed until just incorporated. Mix in the chocolate. Transfer bowl to refrigerator; chill dough 1 hour.

3. Heat oven to 400°. Line three baking sheets with parchment, and set aside.

4. Roll ¼ cup dough into a ball, and place on a baking sheet. Repeat, placing a total of four balls on each sheet. Chill 20 minutes.

5. Transfer two baking sheets to oven, and bake 7 minutes. Rotate pans, and continue baking until just brown around edges, 6 to 8 minutes. Transfer baking sheets to wire racks; cool 2 minutes. Transfer cookies to racks, and cool completely.

6. Bake remaining cookies, and cool. Store all cookies in an airtight container up to 2 days.

53 oatmeal-pecan chocolate-chunk cookies

2 cups all-purpose flour
½ teaspoon salt
1 teaspoon baking powder
1 teaspoon baking soda
1 cup (2 sticks) unsalted butter,
  room temperature
1 cup packed light-brown sugar
1 cup granulated sugar
1 tablespoon pure vanilla extract
3 tablespoons milk
2 large eggs
3 cups old-fashioned oats
12 ounces semisweet chocolate,
  chopped into ½-inch chunks
1⅓ cups (5 ounces) coarsely
  chopped pecans

You can substitute raisins for the chocolate chunks. | **makes about 2 dozen**

1. In a medium bowl, whisk together flour, salt, baking powder, and baking soda. Set aside.

2. In the bowl of an electric mixer fitted with the paddle attachment, combine the butter with both sugars; beat until light and fluffy. Add the vanilla, milk, and eggs; mix well. Add the reserved dry ingredients, and beat until just combined. Remove bowl from mixer, and fold in the oats, chocolate, and pecans. Place dough in the refrigerator until firm, at least 2 hours or overnight.

3. Heat oven to 350°. Line two baking sheets with parchment paper, and set aside.

4. Remove dough from refrigerator. Using an ice-cream scoop, shape dough into 2-inch balls. Place six balls on each baking sheet, spaced 4 inches apart. Press down, flattening balls into 3-inch disks.

5. Transfer baking sheets to oven. Bake until golden, but still soft in center, 15 to 16 minutes. Transfer to a wire rack to cool completely. Repeat with the remaining dough. Store all cookies in an airtight container up to 2 days.

54 big ginger cookies

2 ½ cups all-purpose flour
2 ¼ teaspoons baking soda
½ teaspoon salt
1 tablespoon ground ginger
½ teaspoon ground allspice
½ teaspoon ground white pepper
1 cup (2 sticks) plus 2 tablespoons unsalted butter
½ cup packed light-brown sugar
½ cup granulated sugar
6 tablespoons unsulfured molasses
1 large egg
½ cup sanding or granulated sugar

Sanding sugar, which is coarser than granulated sugar, adds sparkle to these soft, chewy cookies. Before putting the cookies in the oven, use the bottom of a drinking glass to flatten them. | **makes 1 dozen**

1. Heat oven to 350°. Line two baking sheets with parchment paper, and set aside.

2. In a medium bowl, whisk together flour, baking soda, salt, ginger, allspice, and white pepper.

3. In bowl of an electric mixer fitted with the paddle attachment, combine the butter with the light-brown and granulated sugars until light and fluffy. Beat in the molasses and egg; mix well. Add the reserved dry ingredients, and beat just until combined. Form dough into a ball, and wrap in plastic. Chill until firm, at least 2 hours or overnight.

4. Remove dough from refrigerator. Using an ice-cream scoop, shape dough into 2-inch balls. Pour sanding sugar into a large bowl, and roll each ball in the sanding sugar, coating well. Place coated balls on prepared baking sheets, spaced 4 inches apart. Flatten each into a 3-inch disk.

5. Transfer baking sheets to oven, and bake until brown, 12 to 15 minutes. Remove from oven, and transfer to a wire rack to cool. Store cookies in an airtight container up to 2 days.

55 shortbread

2 cups (4 sticks) unsalted butter, cut into small pieces, plus more for pans
1 cup firmly packed light-brown sugar
5 cups all-purpose flour
1 teaspoon salt

For ginger-flavored shortbread, mix:
1 heaping tablespoon candied ginger, finely chopped
1 teaspoon ground ginger
¼ teaspoon ground white pepper

For orange-flavored shortbread, mix:
1 heaping tablespoon candied orange peel (see the Guide), finely chopped
Zest of 1 orange, grated
1 tablespoon Grand Marnier liqueur

Unlike most cookies, shortbread improves with age. It can be stored in an airtight container for up to two weeks before serving. Before the holidays, consider making all three flavors for gifts. | **makes three 8-inch rounds**

1. Heat oven to 275°. Butter three 8-by-2-inch round cake pans, and line bottoms with parchment.

2. In the bowl of an electric mixer fitted with the paddle attachment, cream butter and sugar on high speed until light and fluffy, about 2 minutes. Add flour, 1 cup at a time, beating on low speed until just combined. Add salt, and combine.

3. Divide dough into three equal parts, and transfer two of them to separate bowls. If desired, add ginger flavoring to one bowl, and add the orange flavoring to another. Mix in flavorings until combined.

4. Transfer each batch of dough to a prepared pan, leveling and smoothing tops. Using a dough scraper (right) or the back of a knife, lightly score batter into wedges. Using the tines of a fork or a wooden skewer, create a decorative pattern on the surface.

5. Bake shortbread until pale golden, but not browned, 45 to 50 minutes. Transfer to a wire rack to cool, 10 minutes. Run a knife around inside pans to loosen shortbread, and turn out. Remove parchment, and turn over. Using a serrated knife, follow the score marks to cut shortbread into neat wedges.

56 key-lime sablés

1⅓ cups flour, plus more for
    rolling out dough

⅓ cup confectioners' sugar,
    plus more for dusting

1½ tablespoons granulated sugar

¼ teaspoon coarse salt

¾ cup (1½ sticks) unsalted butter,
    chilled and cut into pieces

1½ teaspoons pure lime extract
    Key-Lime Curd (recipe follows)

Use square cookie cutters to prepare these; bake the cut-out windows for extra nibbles. | **makes 2 dozen**

1. Place flour, confectioners' sugar, granulated sugar, and salt in bowl of a food processor. Pulse until well combined. Add butter; pulse until coarse crumbs form. Add lime extract; pulse to mix.

2. Transfer the dough to a clean work surface, and flatten, forming a disk. Wrap the dough in plastic, and transfer to refrigerator. Chill until very firm, at least 2 hours.

3. Heat oven to 325°. Line a baking sheet with a Silpat baking mat (see the Guide); set aside.

4. On a lightly floured surface, roll out the dough to an ⅛-inch thickness. Using a 1¾-inch fluted cookie cutter, cut the dough into squares. Using a 1-inch fluted cutter, cut windows from half of the squares. Place squares on the prepared baking sheet, spaced about 1 inch apart.

5. Bake until just golden, 15 to 17 minutes. Transfer to a wire rack to cool completely.

6. To assemble the sandwiches, spread 1 teaspoon lime curd on the bottom of the full squares. Dust the cut-out squares with confectioners' sugar, then place on top of the curd, forming little sandwiches. Refrigerate until firm, about 20 minutes. Serve.

key-lime curd | **makes ¾ cup**

½ cup sugar

2 large eggs, lightly beaten

¼ cup freshly squeezed key-lime
    juice plus 2 teaspoons grated
    zest (6 limes)

4 tablespoons unsalted butter,
    cut into small pieces

1. Combine sugar, eggs, lime juice, and zest in a medium nonreactive saucepan. Set over medium-low heat; cook, whisking constantly, until mixture thickens and holds the mark of whisk, about 20 minutes.

2. Remove from heat; whisk in butter, a piece at a time, until well combined. Strain through a sieve into a glass bowl. Lay plastic wrap directly on surface to prevent a skin from forming. Chill 3 hours.

57 lemon-drop wafers

4 tablespoons unsalted butter,
    room temperature

1½ cups sugar

1 large egg
    Zest of 2 lemons, finely chopped

⅔ cup all-purpose flour

¼ teaspoon baking soda
    Pinch of salt

⅓ cup lemon drops, crushed
    (2 ounces whole candies)

The crushed candy adds a lemony crunch to these easy-to-make cookies. | **makes about 2 dozen**

1. Heat oven to 350°. Line two baking sheets with Silpat baking mats (see the Guide), and set aside.

2. In the bowl of an electric mixer fitted with the paddle attachment, cream butter and 1 cup sugar until light and fluffy, 3 to 5 minutes, scraping down sides of bowl twice. Add the egg; mix on high speed until combined. Add lemon zest, and beat to combine.

3. In a large bowl, whisk together flour, baking soda, and salt. Add to butter mixture, and mix on medium-low speed until combined, about 20 seconds. Add candy, and mix to combine. Transfer dough to a sheet of plastic wrap. Freeze until firm, about 30 minutes.

4. Pour the remaining ½ cup sugar into a large bowl. Shape the dough into ½-inch balls. Drop each ball into sugar, and roll, coating completely; use sugar to keep dough from sticking to hands.

5. Working in batches, place sugared balls on prepared baking sheets, spaced 2 inches apart. Gently press balls, flattening to a ¼-inch thickness. Transfer remaining dough to refrigerator.

6. Bake cookies just until golden, about 10 minutes. Transfer to a wire rack to cool. Repeat with the remaining dough. Store in an airtight container up to 2 weeks.

56 & 57

A very pretty cookie sandwich is created from a basic butter cookie and key-lime curd, making a tart, crumbly concoction complex in texture and flavor. Both the key-lime sablés and the round lemon-drop wafers behind them are unbeatable with a freshly made, appropriately bitter cup of coffee. The teacup and plate are early-nineteenth-century gilt-trimmed Wedgwood drabware.

59 *There are many variations on the classic chocolate brownie, but we think this is the best. Incredibly versatile, brownies are suitable as an after-school snack, an offering at a bake sale, or a casual dinner-party dessert, dressed up with a scoop of vanilla or mint chocolate-chip ice cream. These brownies get their complex texture from walnuts and chocolate chips, and their deep, intense flavor from the addition of some espresso. The light-blue pressed-glass dessert plate is Fire King from the fifties; the ice cream is served in Victorian gothic-panel ironstone syllabub cups.*

58 cranberry-lemon squares

6 tablespoons cold unsalted
butter, cut into 12 pieces,
plus more for pan

1½ cups dried cranberries
(about 7 ounces; available at
specialty-food stores)

¼ cup confectioners' sugar,
plus more for dusting

1 cup all-purpose flour

2 large eggs

¾ cup granulated sugar

¼ cup plus 1½ teaspoons freshly
squeezed lemon juice
(about 3 lemons)

These tart bars use dried cranberries instead of fresh, so you can make them any time of year. | **makes about 16**

1. Heat oven to 325°. Butter an 8-inch square baking pan, and set aside.

2. In a medium saucepan, combine cranberries and 2 cups water; bring to a boil. Reduce heat to medium, and cook, stirring occasionally, until water has been absorbed, about 25 minutes.

3. Transfer cranberry mixture to bowl of a food processor; chop coarsely. Transfer to a bowl, and set aside.

4. In bowl of an electric mixer fitted with paddle attachment, combine confectioners' sugar and ¼ cup flour. Add the butter, beating on low speed until mixture forms pea-size pieces. Press batter into baking pan.

5. Bake until golden, about 20 minutes. Transfer to a wire rack to cool.

6. Beat eggs and granulated sugar until smooth. Add lemon juice; beat to combine. Add remaining ¼ cup flour, and beat to combine; set lemon mixture aside.

7. Reduce oven temperature to 300°. Spread cranberry mixture over cooked crust. Pour lemon mixture over the cranberry mixture. Bake until set, about 40 minutes. Transfer to a wire rack to cool, 40 minutes. Chill 4 hours. To serve, cut into squares and dust with confectioners' sugar.

59 chocolate brownies

1 cup coarsely chopped
walnuts (optional)

1 cup (2 sticks) unsalted butter,
plus more for pan

8 ounces best-quality unsweetened
chocolate, such as Callebaut
or Valrhona

5 large eggs

3½ cups sugar

2 teaspoons instant espresso

1 tablespoon pure vanilla extract

1⅔ cups sifted all-purpose flour

½ teaspoon salt

½ cup semisweet chocolate chips

Always remember: The better the chocolate, the better the brownie. | **makes 1 dozen**

1. Heat oven to 350°. Spread the chopped walnuts on a baking pan; toast until fragrant, 5 to 10 minutes. Transfer nuts to a bowl to cool.

2. Increase oven temperature to 400°. Generously butter a 9-by-13-inch baking pan; set aside.

3. Combine the chocolate and butter in a heat-proof bowl or the top of a double boiler. Set over a pan of simmering water until the chocolate mixture has melted. Remove from heat; set aside.

4. In the bowl of an electric mixer fitted with the paddle attachment, beat the eggs, sugar, and espresso at high speed, 10 minutes. Reduce speed to low, and add the melted-chocolate mixture and the vanilla; beat until combined. Slowly add the flour and salt; beat just until incorporated. Fold in the chocolate chips and toasted walnuts. Pour the batter into the prepared pan.

5. Bake until edges are dry but center is still soft, about 35 minutes. Remove pan from oven, and transfer to a wire rack to cool. Cut into 3-inch squares, and store in an airtight container up to 2 days.

60 sand tarts

8 tablespoons (1 stick)
   unsalted butter
1 cup sugar
2 large eggs, separated
1 teaspoon pure vanilla extract
1 teaspoon lemon zest, chopped
2½ cups sifted all-purpose flour
¼ teaspoon salt
   Sliced almonds, for decorating
   Cinnamon sugar, for sprinkling

Decorate these crisp sugar cookies with sliced almonds to make them look like sand dollars. | **makes 2 dozen**

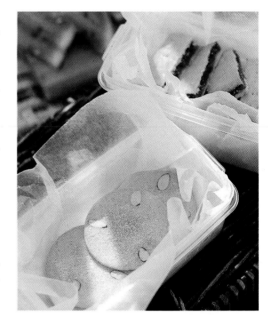

1. In the bowl of an electric mixer fitted with paddle attachment, cream the butter until fluffy. Gradually add the sugar, and beat until light in color. Beat in 2 egg yolks, 1 egg white, vanilla, and lemon zest.

2. In a medium bowl, sift together flour and salt; add to butter mixture. Mix just until dough comes together. Wrap in plastic, and chill 2 hours.

3. Heat oven to 400°. In a small bowl, combine remaining egg white and 1 teaspoon water. Set egg wash aside.

4. Roll out dough to an ⅛-inch thickness. Using a 3½-inch-round cookie cutter, cut out cookies; place on an ungreased baking sheet. Brush with egg wash, and decorate each with 3 sliced almonds. Sprinkle cinnamon sugar over tops.

5. Bake until golden brown, 8 to 10 minutes. Transfer the baking sheet to a wire rack and set aside until cookies are cool. Store cookies in an airtight container up to 2 days.

61 fig bars

2 sticks (1 cup) unsalted butter,
   room temperature
½ cup sugar
1 large whole egg
2 large egg yolks
1 teaspoon pure vanilla extract
   Zest of 1 lemon
2½ cups all-purpose flour
   Pinch of salt
   Fig Filling (recipe follows)

This homemade version of the supermarket standby (shown above, with the sand tarts) keeps well in an airtight container. | **makes 2 dozen**

1. In the bowl of an electric mixer fitted with the paddle attachment, cream the butter and sugar. Add the whole egg, 1 egg yolk, vanilla, and lemon zest; mix well. Add flour and salt; mix on low speed just until dough comes together. Wrap dough in plastic, and chill until firm, about 1 hour.

2. Divide dough in half. Roll out one half to fit a 10-by-15-inch baking sheet. Pick up dough by wrapping it around a rolling pin, and unroll it onto baking sheet.

3. Spread fig filling evenly over the pastry. Roll out remaining half of dough, and cover filling. Trim any excess pastry, making an even rectangle. Transfer baking sheet to refrigerator, and chill 1 hour.

4. Heat oven to 375°. In a bowl, combine remaining egg yolk and 1 teaspoon water. Set egg wash aside.

5. Use a paring knife, score dough lightly into 1-by-3-inch bars. Use a fork to prick holes in each bar. Lightly brush with egg wash. Bake until golden brown, 25 to 30 minutes. Cut into bars, and let cool. Store in an airtight container up to 2 days.

fig filling

3   cups chopped dried
    Calimyrna figs,
¼   cup honey
1   cup red wine
¼   teaspoon cinnamon
½   teaspoon finely ground pepper

Combine all ingredients with 1 cup water in a medium saucepan. Cook over low heat, stirring often, until reduced to a thick paste, about 10 to 15 minutes. Spread the filling on a baking sheet to cool.

62 chocolate-mint wafers

½   cup (1 stick) unsalted butter,
    room temperature
½   cup sugar
1   large egg, room temperature
1   cup cocoa powder
½   cup plus 2 tablespoons
    all-purpose flour
    Confectioners' sugar, for
    rolling out dough
¼   cup heavy cream
6   ounces semisweet chocolate
2   to 3 drops peppermint
    oil or ½ teaspoon pure
    peppermint extract

If you adore the combination of chocolate and mint, this may become your favorite cookie. | **makes about 3 dozen**

1. In the bowl of an electric mixer fitted with paddle attachment, cream butter and sugar until completely smooth, about 3 minutes. Add the egg, and continue mixing until well combined.

2. In a medium bowl, whisk together the cocoa powder and the flour.

3. Add flour mixture to batter; mix until combined, scraping down sides of bowl once. Divide dough in half; wrap each half in plastic. Flatten each ball into a disk; chill until firm, at least 1 hour.

4. Heat the oven to 350°. Line two baking sheets with Silpat baking mats (see the Guide) or parchment. Set prepared pans aside.

5. Lightly sprinkle a clean work surface with confectioners' sugar. Roll out dough to an ⅛-inch thickness. Using a 2-inch cookie cutter, cut out cookies, and transfer to prepared baking sheets, spaced ½ inch apart. Chill any trimmings, and roll out again.

6. Bake the cookies until you can smell the chocolate, about 12 minutes. Transfer the baking sheets to a wire rack to cool.

7. Bring cream to a boil in a small saucepan set over medium-high heat. Chop chocolate very finely, and add to hot cream. Stir with a rubber spatula until the chocolate has melted and mixture is smooth. Add peppermint oil. Remove from heat; let ganache cool slightly, 10 to 15 minutes.

8. Transfer ganache to a resealable plastic bag; seal, and cut off one corner at an angle. Pipe about 1 teaspoon onto the center of half of the wafers. Top with the remaining wafers. Chill the assembled cookies until firm, about 10 minutes. Store in an airtight container up to 2 days.

63 three macaroons

coconut macaroons | makes 20

Unsweetened coconut, which is available in health-food stores, is essential to all three variations of these cookies.

1. Heat oven to 350°. Line a baking sheet with parchment paper.

2. In a large bowl, combine sugar, coconut, egg whites, vanilla, and salt. Using your hands, mix well, completely combining ingredients.

3. Dampen hands with cold water. Form 1½ tablespoons of mixture into a loose haystack shape; place on prepared baking sheet. Repeat with remaining mixture, spacing about 1 inch apart.

4. Bake until golden brown, about 15 minutes. Transfer baking sheet to a wire rack to cool. Store macaroons in an airtight container up to 3 days.

¾ cup sugar
2½ cups unsweetened shredded coconut
2 large egg whites
1 teaspoon pure vanilla extract
Pinch of salt

chocolate-chunk macaroons | makes 20

For this version, you can use chocolate chunks, chocolate chips, or even broken pieces of your favorite chocolate bar.

1. Heat oven to 350°. Line a baking sheet with parchment paper.

2. In a large bowl, combine sugar, coconut, egg whites, chocolate chunks, vanilla, and salt. Using your hands, mix well, completely combining ingredients.

3. Dampen hands with cold water. Form 1½ tablespoons of mixture into a loose haystack shape; place on prepared baking sheet. Repeat with remaining mixture, spacing about 1 inch apart.

4. Bake until golden brown, about 15 to 20 minutes. Transfer baking sheet to a wire rack to cool. Leave in a warm place 1 hour, allowing chocolate to soften. Store in an airtight container up to 3 days.

¾ cup sugar
2½ cups unsweetened shredded coconut
2 large egg whites
½ cup semisweet chocolate chunks (about 3 ounces)
1 teaspoon pure vanilla extract
Pinch of salt

chocolate macaroons | makes 2 dozen

1. Heat oven to 350°. Line a baking sheet with parchment paper.

2. Place chocolate in a heat-proof bowl or the top of a double boiler, and set over a pan of simmering water. Stir until chocolate has melted, and set aside to cool.

3. In a large bowl, combine cooled chocolate, cocoa, sugar, coconut, egg whites, vanilla, and salt. Using your hands, mix well, completely combining ingredients.

4. Dampen hands with cold water. Form 1½ tablespoons of mixture into a loose haystack shape; place on prepared baking sheet. Repeat with remaining mixture, spacing about 1 inch apart.

5. Bake until just firm to the touch but still soft in the middle, 15 to 20 minutes. Transfer baking sheet to a wire rack to cool. Store macaroons in an airtight container up to 3 days.

4 ounces semisweet chocolate, broken into small pieces
¼ cup unsweetened cocoa, sifted
¾ cup sugar
2½ cups unsweetened shredded coconut
3 large egg whites
1 teaspoon pure vanilla extract
Pinch of salt

63 *Macaroons are chewy coconut cookies that are well suited to variations. On the top plate are chocolate macaroons; on the middle, the classic coconut; and on the bottom, chocolate chunk. It is traditional to serve macaroons on the Jewish holiday of Passover, when no leavening agents can be used, but, of course, they are good anytime.*

64 *This simple yet
spectacular dessert is perfect for
a spring or summer party. It
combines the intense flavors and
colors of four fruit sorbets — green
apple, raspberry, pink grapefruit,
and mango — with disks of delicate,
snowy meringue. We stopped at
four, but brave souls could keep
going. Because meringues crumble
when cut, this cake's majesty soon
becomes a memory, so be sure
that everyone has a chance to
view its moment of beauty.*

chapter six

Frozen Desserts

Everyone loves ice
cream — in a bowl, cone,
or cake. Ready to
choose your flavors?

On a hot summer day, is anything as satisfying as ice cream? No food is more fun to eat, to swirl and twirl, as it melts, creamy and sweet. * The ancient Chinese relied only on mountain snow and fruit juice to create the first frozen desserts more than two thousand years ago. The Persians elaborated by adding flower essences: rose, violet, and gardenia were popular. And the

Victorians made an art of ice cream by using metal molds to shape it into fruit, flowers, baskets, even artichokes and fish. * The passion for tinkering with frozen concoctions continues in our kitchens today. Making ice cream requires no special skills, just patience and an ice-cream maker. Try making gelato, smooth Italian ice cream with an intense taste, in one of our six flavors. Or, using store-bought or homemade ice cream, create an ice-cream cake. Our rainbow sorbet cake is as pretty and colorful as a summer garden. And although ice cream is truly the magic food of summer, ice-cream cakes can be year-round pleasures. Our frozen "tiramisu," with its coffee flavors, would be a fitting end to a cozy winter dinner. * Our ice-cream cakes are easy to make. In general, you use your freezer in stages, chilling layers one by one. The process can't be rushed, so don't cut corners. The trick is in getting the ice cream to the right consistency—spreadable but not melting—by beating it in a mixer or softening it and beating by hand. Substitutions are encouraged: Use your favorite flavors, or change the shape or size (just don't make a cake that's too big). Most of these desserts should be frozen until completely hardened—at least two hours but as long as overnight. Before serving, soften the cake in the refrigerator for about thirty minutes. Use a sharp knife, dipped in hot water and wiped dry, to slice the cake. * A scoop of ice cream is a joy on any day, but if it's a special day, why not make a whole cake of it? It's the ultimate good-time dessert.

64 rainbow sorbet cake

1½ cups sugar

6 large egg whites

⅔ pint mango sorbet

⅔ pint grapefruit sorbet
   (see the Guide)

⅔ pint raspberry sorbet

⅔ pint green-apple sorbet
   (see the Guide)

For this lofty layer cake, you can use any sorbet flavors you like; we chose these for the combination of flavors and colors. The meringue disks (steps one through five) can be made up to five days ahead and stored in an airtight container until you're ready to assemble the cake. Because the sorbet does not have to be softened or spread smoothly, this cake is quick to put together. | **serves 10**

1. Heat oven to 185°. Cut 10-inch square of ¼-inch-thick cardboard or Foamcore, and cut a 7-inch circle from the square. Set circle aside to use for bottom of cake, and reserve the cut-out square as a template. Cut three 11-by-17-inch rectangles out of parchment paper, and set parchment aside.

2. Fill a medium saucepan with 2 inches of water, and bring to a simmer. Place the sugar and egg whites in the heat-proof bowl of an electric mixer. Hold bowl over simmering water, and whisk until warm to the touch and sugar has dissolved, about 3 minutes.

3. Using the whisk attachment, beat egg whites on medium speed until stiff and glossy, about 4 minutes, being careful not to overbeat.

4. Place the template over one end of a piece of parchment. Scoop 1 cup egg-white mixture into the center. Using an offset spatula, spread the mixture into an even layer. Remove the template. Make another disk on other end of parchment. Create three more disks on remaining two pieces of parchment. Slide each piece of parchment onto a 11-by-17-inch baking sheet.

5. Transfer the baking sheets to the oven, and bake disks 1½ hours, making sure they don't brown. Turn off heat, and let the disks dry completely in oven, 6 hours to overnight.

6. Place one meringue disk on the reserved 7-inch cake round. Using a gelato paddle or a large spoon, build up an even layer of mango sorbet on top of the disk. Top with a second meringue disk. Continue the layering process, using remaining grapefruit, raspberry, and green-apple sorbets and the meringue disks. Top with a disk. Transfer cake to freezer, and freeze until completely hardened.

65 *Our frozen version of the popular Italian dessert tiramisu is a coffee lover's dream, combining a simple sponge cake soaked in espresso-Kahlúa syrup, espresso and coffee ice creams, layers of finely ground espresso, all topped off with chocolate curls. These very adult flavors make it sophisticated enough to serve at an elegant dinner party.*

65 frozen "tiramisu"

1 cup sugar
1½ cups strong, freshly
 brewed espresso
⅓ cup Kahlúa liqueur (optional)
 Vanilla Sponge Cake
 (recipe follows)
¼ cup finely ground espresso
2 pints espresso ice cream
 (see the Guide)
2 pints coffee ice cream
 Chocolate Curls (recipe follows)

Cut this cake into squares right in the pan, and serve on dessert plates or in café-au-lait bowls. When shopping, look for two different flavors or styles of coffee ice cream. | **serves 12**

1. Place sugar and ⅔ cup water in a small saucepan. Bring to a boil over medium heat, stirring occasionally. Remove from heat; stir in brewed espresso and Kahlúa. Let the syrup cool.

2. Using a serrated knife, cut the sponge cake in half horizontally, making two layers. Place one layer in the bottom of a 9-by-9-by-2-inch baking pan. Using a pastry brush, brush with ¾ cup cooled syrup. Sift 2 tablespoons ground espresso over the cake.

3. Place the espresso ice cream in the bowl of an electric mixer. Beat on low speed with the paddle attachment until spreadable. Spread ice cream over cake; top with second layer of sponge cake. Brush with remaining syrup. Transfer cake to freezer, 20 minutes.

4. Remove cake from freezer; sprinkle with remaining 2 tablespoons ground espresso. Place coffee ice cream in mixer bowl. Beat on low speed until spreadable. Spread ice cream over cake, forming large swirls. Freeze until completely hardened. When ready to serve, garnish with chocolate curls.

vanilla sponge cake | makes one 9-inch-square cake

1 tablespoon unsalted butter,
 for pan
½ cup all-purpose flour, plus
 more for pan
½ cup cornstarch
4 large eggs, separated
1 teaspoon pure vanilla extract
¾ cup sugar
 Pinch of salt

This cake also makes a wonderful base for strawberry or peach shortcake. Just sprinkle sugar on sliced fruit, and let the fruit sit; then spoon fruit over the cake and top with homemade whipped cream.

1. Heat oven to 350°. Butter a 9-inch-square baking pan. Line bottom of pan with parchment; butter again. Flour the pan, and set aside. In a small bowl, sift together the flour and cornstarch; set aside.

2. In the bowl of an electric mixer fitted with the whisk attachment, beat the egg yolks, vanilla, and ½ cup sugar on high speed until thick and pale, about 5 minutes. Transfer the egg-yolk mixture to a large bowl. Wash and dry the mixer bowl and the whisk attachment.

3. Combine the egg whites and salt in the mixer bowl, and beat on medium speed until whites hold soft peaks, about 1½ minutes. With mixer running, slowly add the remaining ¼ cup sugar. Continue beating until stiff and glossy, about 1 minute.

4. Fold the egg-white mixture into the egg-yolk mixture. In three additions, fold the reserved flour mixture into this new mixture. Transfer the batter to the pan, and smooth the top with an offset spatula.

5. Bake until a cake tester inserted into middle comes out clean, 35 to 40 minutes. Transfer pan to a wire rack to cool. Turn out the cake, and wrap in plastic until ready to use. Store up to 2 days.

chocolate curls | makes 8 ounces

8 ounces semisweet or bittersweet
 chocolate, chopped into
 ½-inch pieces
1 teaspoon vegetable shortening

1. Set a heat-proof bowl or the top of a double boiler over a pan of barely simmering water. Melt chocolate and shortening in bowl, stirring occasionally.

2. Divide chocolate between two flat, smooth 11-by-17-inch baking pans; spread evenly with an offset spatula. Chill until your finger makes a mark but not a hole when touching the chocolate.

3. Remove pans from refrigerator. Hold a sturdy metal pancake spatula at a forty-five-degree angle to pan; scrape away from you, forming curls. If chocolate is too brittle, quickly wave pan over warm stove. If too soft, briefly return to refrigerator. Refrigerate in an airtight container up to 2 weeks.

66 *To make gelato, the ice cream of Italy, flavorings are infused into milk before it is used to make the custard base — the result is a wonderfully intense flavor. While denser than American ice cream, gelato seems more refreshing, its strong flavors not muted by an excess of butterfat. On this page are five classic flavors ready for tasting: Clockwise from top left are blood-orange gelato, which evokes childhood memories of Creamsicles; coconut; hazelnut; pistachio; and ricotta. Opposite is mint chocolate-chip gelato.*

66 six gelati

coconut gelato | makes about 1 quart

1 fresh coconut (about 12 ounces)
3 cups whole milk
5 large egg yolks
½ cup sugar
½ cup heavy cream
½ cup cream of coconut
(see the Guide)
½ cup sweetened angel-flake
coconut

1. Puncture the eyes of the coconut with a nail, and drain the milk into a small saucepan. Using a hammer, crack open the coconut. Remove the outer shell and dark-brown skin; discard. Grate flesh.

2. Cook coconut milk over low heat until reduced to syrup consistency, about 20 minutes. Set aside.

3. In a large saucepan, combine the whole milk and grated coconut. Bring to a gentle boil, cover, and remove pan from heat. Let steep 1 hour. Pass mixture through a cheesecloth-lined sieve, pressing very hard on solids. Reserve strained whole milk, and discard solids.

4. Combine egg yolks and sugar in the bowl of an electric mixer fitted with paddle attachment. Cream at medium-high speed until very thick and pale yellow, 3 to 5 minutes. Return whole milk to a simmer.

5. Add half of the warm whole milk to egg-yolk mixture, and whisk until blended. Return new mixture to saucepan with remaining milk. Cook over low heat, stirring constantly, until the mixture is thick enough to coat the back of a wooden spoon.

6. Have ready an ice-water bath. Remove saucepan from heat, and immediately stir in the cream. Pass mixture through a sieve set over a medium bowl. Place bowl in ice-water bath, and chill. Add the reduced coconut milk and the cream of coconut.

7. Freeze in an ice-cream maker according to the manufacturer's instructions. Add the sweetened coconut flakes, and mix in machine until combined, about 30 seconds. Store in an airtight container.

pistachio gelato | makes about 1 quart

2 cups shelled pistachios
(½ pound)
3 cups whole milk
5 large egg yolks
⅔ cup sugar
1 cup heavy cream

1. Heat oven to 350°. Bring a saucepan of water to a boil. Add pistachios, and cook 30 seconds. Drain pistachios. When cool enough to handle, remove outer skins; discard. Spread nuts on a baking sheet, and toast in oven 5 minutes. Let cool completely, then coarsely grind.

2. Combine milk and ground pistachios in a medium saucepan. Bring to a gentle boil, cover, and remove pan from heat. Let steep 2 hours. Pass through a cheesecloth-lined sieve, pressing hard on solids. Reserve strained milk, and discard solids.

3. Combine egg yolks and sugar in the bowl of an electric mixer fitted with paddle attachment. Cream at medium-high speed until very thick and pale yellow, 3 to 5 minutes. Return the milk to a simmer.

4. Add half of the warm milk to egg-yolk mixture, and whisk until blended. Return new mixture to saucepan with remaining milk. Cook over low heat, stirring constantly, until mixture is thick enough to coat the back of a wooden spoon.

5. Have ready an ice-water bath. Remove saucepan from heat, and immediately stir in the cream. Pass mixture through a sieve set over a medium bowl. Place bowl in ice-water bath, and chill.

6. Freeze in an ice-cream maker according to manufacturer's instructions. Store in airtight container.

hazelnut gelato | makes about 1 quart

Follow recipe for Pistachio Gelato (above), but substitute unblanched hazelnuts for the pistachios. Toast 8 to 10 minutes, and remove skins. Stir in 1 tablespoon Frangelico liqueur before freezing.

blood-orange gelato | makes about 1 quart

2 cups whole milk
Zest of 1 blood orange
plus 1 cup freshly squeezed
blood-orange juice
(about 4 oranges)
5 large egg yolks
¾ cup sugar
1 cup heavy cream

1. In a medium saucepan, combine milk and orange zest. Bring to a gentle boil, cover, and remove pan from heat. Let steep 30 minutes.

2. In a small saucepan, cook orange juice over medium-low heat until reduced by three-fourths, 30 to 40 minutes. Remove pan from heat, and let orange syrup cool completely.

3. Combine egg yolks and sugar in the bowl of an electric mixer fitted with the paddle attachment. Cream at medium-high speed until very thick and pale yellow, 3 to 5 minutes. Return milk to a simmer.

4. Add half of warm milk to egg-yolk mixture; whisk until blended. Return new mixture to saucepan. Cook over low heat, stirring constantly, until thick enough to coat back of a wooden spoon.

5. Have ready an ice-water bath. Remove saucepan from heat; immediately stir in cream. Pass mixture through a sieve set over a medium bowl. Place bowl in ice-water bath; chill. Stir in orange syrup.

6. Freeze in ice-cream maker according to manufacturer's instructions. Store in an airtight container.

ricotta gelato | makes about 1 quart

2 cups fresh ricotta cheese
2 cups whole milk
¼ teaspoon ground nutmeg
5 large egg yolks
1 cup sugar
1 cup heavy cream

1. Place ricotta in a cheesecloth-lined sieve set over a bowl. Place in refrigerator, and drain overnight.

2. Combine milk and nutmeg in a medium saucepan; bring to a simmer.

3. Combine egg yolks and sugar in the bowl of an electric mixer fitted with the paddle attachment. Cream at medium-high speed until very thick and pale yellow, 3 to 5 minutes.

4. Add half of the warm milk to the egg-yolk mixture; whisk until blended. Return new mixture to saucepan with remaining milk. Cook over low heat, stirring constantly, until the mixture is thick enough to coat the back of a wooden spoon.

5. Have ready an ice-water bath. Remove saucepan from heat, and immediately stir in the cream. Pass mixture through a sieve set over a medium bowl. Place bowl in ice-water bath, and chill. Whisk in drained ricotta until thoroughly blended.

6. Freeze in an ice-cream maker according to manufacturer's instructions. Store in an airtight container.

mint chocolate-chip gelato | makes about 1 quart

2½ cups whole milk
14 sprigs fresh mint
5 large egg yolks
⅔ cup sugar
1 cup heavy cream
¼ teaspoon pure peppermint
extract
4 ounces semisweet chocolate,
chopped

1. In a medium saucepan, combine milk and 12 sprigs mint. Bring to a gentle boil, cover, and remove pan from heat. Let steep 30 minutes. Strain mixture; reserve milk, and discard solids.

2. Combine egg yolks and sugar in the bowl of an electric mixer fitted with paddle attachment. Beat at medium-high speed until very thick and pale yellow, 3 to 5 minutes. Return milk to a simmer.

3. Add half of the warm milk to egg-yolk mixture; whisk until blended. Return new mixture to saucepan with remaining milk. Cook over low heat, stirring constantly, until the mixture is thick enough to coat the back of a wooden spoon.

4. Have ready an ice-water bath. Remove saucepan from heat; immediately stir in cream. Pass mixture through a sieve set over a medium bowl. Place bowl in ice-water bath; chill. Stir in peppermint.

5. Freeze in ice-cream maker according to instructions. Finely chop remaining 2 sprigs mint. Add mint and chocolate; mix in machine until combined, about 30 seconds. Store in an airtight container.

67 mint chocolate-chip cake

Dark-Chocolate Cake
(recipe follows)
3 pints green mint chocolate-
chip ice cream
2 pints white mint chocolate-
chip ice cream

This is a great cake to make with anyone who enjoys nibbling while cooking, because you have to trim the layers twice, leaving some wonderful pieces of cake and ice cream. | **serves 8**

1. Trim chocolate cake layers to six-inch squares. Slice each layer in half horizontally, making a total of four layers. Cut a 6-inch square of cardboard or Foamcore; set aside.

2. Microwave the green ice cream until softened, about 20 seconds. Transfer ice cream to a medium mixing bowl, and stir with a rubber spatula. Place in the freezer. Microwave white ice cream until softened, about 20 seconds, and transfer to another mixing bowl. Stir with a rubber spatula.

3. Place one cake layer on the cardboard. Using an offset spatula, spread 2 cups white ice cream over the cake. Place another cake layer on top of ice cream. Place cake and bowl of white ice cream in the freezer for 20 minutes.

4. Remove the cake and the bowl of green ice cream from freezer. Stir the ice cream with the spatula to soften. Using the spatula, evenly spread 2 cups green ice cream over cake. Place a third cake layer on top. Return the cake and the bowl of green ice cream to the freezer for 20 minutes more.

5. Remove the cake and the bowl of white ice cream from the freezer, and spread the remaining 2 cups white ice cream over the top; place the fourth cake layer on top of the white ice cream. Return the cake to the freezer for 20 minutes more.

6. Remove the cake and bowl of green ice cream from freezer, and spread 2 cups green ice cream over top. Return cake and ice cream to freezer, and chill the cake until firm, about 1 hour.

7. Remove cake and remaining 2 cups green ice cream from freezer. Using a long serrated knife, trim ¼ inch from all sides of cake, making them even. Using an icing spatula, quickly spread remaining green ice cream around sides of cake. Return cake to freezer, and freeze until completely hardened.

dark-chocolate cake | makes two 8-inch-square layers

¾ cup (1½ sticks) unsalted butter, melted, plus more for pans
2 cups all-purpose flour, plus more for pans
1½ cups sugar
¾ cup unsweetened cocoa
½ teaspoon salt
1½ teaspoons baking powder
¾ teaspoon baking soda
1 large whole egg, room temperature
1 large egg white, room temperature
1 teaspoon pure vanilla extract
1⅓ cups strong, hot coffee

1. Heat oven to 325°. Butter two 8-inch-square baking pans. Line with parchment, and butter again. Flour the pans, and set aside.

2. In the bowl of an electric mixer, place all the ingredients except the hot coffee. Using the whisk attachment, mix ingredients on low speed until combined, about 1 minute. Slowly add the coffee. Mix until smooth, about 1 minute. Divide batter between pans; smooth tops with an offset spatula.

3. Bake until a cake tester inserted into the middle of each cake comes out clean, 25 to 30 minutes. Transfer pans to wire rack to cool. Turn out the cakes, and wrap them in plastic wrap until ready to use.

67 *Mint chocolate-chip devotees will relish this dessert. The ice cream serves as both filling and frosting; the sole diversion is dark-chocolate cake enriched with strong coffee. We like alternating layers of green and white mint chocolate-chip ice cream in this striped cake, but you can use just one or the other. The cake is most delectable served thinly sliced.*

68 almond-crunch cake

½ cup granulated sugar

2 tablespoons amaretto liqueur
   (optional)

½ teaspoon pure almond extract
   Almond Sponge Cake
   (recipe follows)

4 pints vanilla ice cream
   Almond Crunch (recipe follows)

¾ cup heavy cream

2 tablespoons confectioners' sugar

Almond fans will never forget this dessert's layers of almond-flavored cake and almond crunch. | **serves 10**

1. Place the granulated sugar and ⅓ cup water in a small saucepan; set over medium heat. Bring to a boil, stirring occasionally. When sugar has dissolved, remove from heat; add the amaretto and the almond extract. Let the syrup cool.

2. Using a serrated knife, slice the two cake layers in half horizontally, forming four layers. Crumble one into a food processor; process until fine crumbs form. Set crumbs aside.

3. Generously brush tops of remaining three cake layers with the cooled syrup. Place one cake layer on a 6-inch cardboard cake round.

4. Place the ice cream in the chilled bowl of an electric mixer fitted with paddle attachment. Beat on medium-low speed until spreadable, about 2 minutes. Spread 2 cups ice cream over first cake layer. Crumble ½ cup almond crunch over ice cream. Top with a second cake layer. Transfer cake and ice cream to freezer until firm, about 10 minutes.

5. Remove cake and ice cream from freezer. Spread 2 cups ice cream over top. Crumble ½ cup almond crunch over ice cream. Place third cake layer on top. Spread 2 cups ice cream over cake layer. Transfer cake and ice cream to freezer for 30 minutes more.

6. Remove cake and ice cream from freezer; stir ice cream with rubber spatula, resoftening it. Using an icing spatula, quickly spread remaining 2 cups ice cream around the sides of cake. Return the cake to the freezer for 30 minutes more.

7. In a chilled bowl, whip cream and confectioners' sugar until soft peaks form. Remove cake from freezer; frost top and sides with whipped cream. Pat reserved cake crumbs onto sides; crumble remaining cup almond crunch over the top. Return cake to freezer; freeze until completely hardened.

almond sponge cake | **makes two 6-inch-round layers**

⅓ cup whole almonds

⅓ cup cornstarch

1 tablespoon unsalted butter,
   for pans

2 tablespoons all-purpose flour,
   for pans

3 large eggs, separated

1 teaspoon pure vanilla extract

½ cup sugar
   Pinch of salt

Toasting the almonds gives this sponge cake a golden color and a nutty flavor.

1. Heat oven to 400°. Place almonds on an ungreased baking sheet, and toast until golden, about 10 minutes. Transfer pan to a wire rack, and let almonds cool.

2. Reduce temperature to 350°. Place the cooled almonds and cornstarch in bowl of a food processor. Process until finely ground, about 30 seconds. Set aside.

3. Butter two 6-inch-round layer-cake pans. Line pans with parchment paper, and butter again. Flour the pans, and set aside.

4. In the bowl of an electric mixer fitted with whisk attachment, mix together egg yolks and vanilla. With mixer on high speed, gradually add ¼ cup sugar. Beat until pale, thick, and light, about 5 minutes. Transfer egg-yolk mixture to a large bowl; set aside. Wash and dry mixer bowl and attachment.

5. Place egg whites and salt in mixer bowl. Beat on medium speed until soft peaks form. Increase the speed to high; gradually add the remaining ¼ cup sugar. Beat until stiff and glossy, about 4 minutes.

6. Fold egg-white mixture into yolk mixture. In three additions, fold reserved ground-almond mixture into new mixture. Divide batter between two prepared pans; smooth tops with an offset spatula.

7. Bake cakes until a cake tester inserted into the middle comes out clean, 25 to 30 minutes. Transfer pans to a wire rack to cool, about 25 minutes. Turn out cakes; wrap in plastic until ready to use.

almond crunch | makes 2 cups

1 cup blanched sliced almonds
6 tablespoons sugar

1. Heat oven to 325°. Have ready a nonstick baking sheet, or place a Silpat (a French nonstick baking mat; see the Guide) on a baking sheet; set aside.

2. In a medium bowl, toss together almonds, sugar, and 2 tablespoons water. Spread almonds evenly over the baking sheet.

3. Bake until golden, about 18 minutes. Transfer pan to a wire rack to cool completely. Store almond crunch in an airtight container until ready to use.

69 coconut bonbons

12 Nabisco Famous
   Chocolate Wafers
½ cup sweetened angel-flake
   coconut, loosely packed
2 pints coconut sorbet
   (see the Guide)
12 whole almonds
26 ounces semisweet or bittersweet
   chocolate, chopped
1 tablespoon vegetable shortening

Beneath their chocolate coatings, these oversize bonbons offer an exciting contrast between a crisp chocolate shell and icy coconut sorbet. After preparing them, melt any excess chocolate that drips onto baking pan, strain it, and reserve for a future use. The bonbons are charming served on porcelain tea saucers (below right). | **makes 12**

1. Set a wire rack over a baking pan. Arrange the wafers, top sides down, on rack, spaced evenly apart. Place 2 teaspoons shredded coconut in the center of each wafer. Using a 2-inch ice-cream scoop, scoop a ball of coconut sorbet onto each wafer. Place an almond on top of each scoop of sorbet (below left). Transfer pan to freezer for 20 minutes.

2. Set a heat-proof bowl or the top of a double boiler over a pan of barely simmering water. Place the chocolate and the shortening in the bowl. Melt mixture, stirring occasionally. Remove bowl from heat. Set aside to cool slightly.

3. Remove baking pan from freezer. Generously ladle melted chocolate over the bonbons (below left), covering bonbons entirely. Return baking pan to the freezer for 30 minutes more, or overnight.

68 *Good Humor's Toasted Almond Bar, a staple of summer, inspired the creation of this extravaganza. Almond cake is brushed with amaretto syrup and then layered with vanilla ice cream and almond crunch. The cake is iced with whipped cream, then coated with cake crumbs and more almonds. A tall cake stand gives it an especially festive lift.*

70 *Anyone who loves pears will buy them in all stages of ripeness, hoping for the moment when both texture and taste are perfect. This dessert is a subtle celebration of that moment. A pear sorbet and a pear ice cream are topped with a pear compote made with brandy, butter, and sugar.*

70 pear ice cream and sorbet with compote

1 tablespoon unsalted butter
4 Bartlett or Anjou pears,
   peeled, cored, and cut
   into 1-inch cubes
2 tablespoons light-brown
   sugar
½ teaspoon ground cinnamon
¼ cup brandy
   Pear Ice Cream (recipe follows)
   Pear Sorbet (recipe follows)

2 cups milk
2 cups heavy cream
1 stick cinnamon
6 Bartlett or Anjou pears,
   peeled, cored, and cut
   into chunks
6 large egg yolks
½ cup sugar
2 tablespoons brandy
   (optional)

This can be assembled at the last minute if the ice cream and sorbet are made ahead. For a pleasing but less time-consuming dessert, serve this lovely compote over best-quality store-bought vanilla ice cream. | **serves 4**

1. Melt butter in a medium sauté pan over medium-high heat. Add pears, and sauté until they start to brown. Add brown sugar and cinnamon; cook 5 minutes more, stirring often.

2. Pour the brandy over pears. Carefully ignite the alcohol, and allow the flame to burn out.

3. To serve, place a scoop of the pear ice cream and a scoop of the pear sorbet in each of four dessert bowls. Divide the warm compote among the bowls. Serve immediately.

pear ice cream | **makes 1 quart**

1. Combine milk, cream, and cinnamon in a medium saucepan; set over medium-low heat. Cook until small bubbles appear around edges. Remove the pan from heat; cover, and let steep 30 minutes.

2. Place pears in a large saucepan, and set over medium-high heat. Cook until a thick sauce forms, about 45 minutes. Remove from heat, and let cool slightly.

3. Transfer pears to a food processor or blender, and purée. Return milk mixture to a simmer.

4. In a small bowl, beat together egg yolks and sugar. Whisk about 1 cup of hot milk mixture into egg mixture. Return new mixture to saucepan with remaining milk mixture. Cook over low heat, stirring constantly, until the ice-cream base is thick enough to coat the back of a wooden spoon, about 5 minutes.

5. Stir pear purée into the ice-cream base. Transfer to refrigerator to chill.

6. Stir in brandy, if using, and freeze in an ice-cream maker according to the manufacturer's instructions. Store in an airtight container.

pear sorbet | **makes 1 quart**

4 Bartlett or Anjou pears,
   peeled, cored, and cut into
   chunks
1 tablespoon freshly squeezed
   lemon juice
1 tablespoon peeled and
   chopped ginger
6 tablespoons sugar

1. Place pear cubes in in a medium saucepan, and sprinkle with lemon juice. Add ginger. Cook over medium heat 10 minutes, stirring occasionally. Add sugar and 1½ cups water; cook, stirring constantly, until sugar has dissolved. Remove pan from heat, and let pears cool slightly.

2. Place pears in the bowl of a food processor or blender, and purée. Transfer purée to a mixing bowl, and refrigerate until chilled.

3. Freeze in an ice-cream maker according to manufacturer's instructions. Store in an airtight container.

71 semifreddo al caffé

6 large egg yolks
½ cup sugar
⅓ cup Kahlúa liqueur
2 tablespoons instant espresso,
 mixed with 2 teaspoons
 hot water
2 cups heavy cream
 Chocolate Sheet Cake
 (recipe follows)
 Coffee Syrup (recipe follows)
 Warm Chocolate Sauce
 (recipe follows)
 Cocoa powder, for dusting

Semifreddo is Italian for "half frozen." | **serves 12 to 16**

1. Place egg yolks in the heat-proof bowl of an electric mixer fitted with the paddle attachment, and beat until pale. Gradually add the sugar; beat until fluffy. Slowly add Kahlúa, and beat until fluffy again.

2. Set the bowl over a pan of barely simmering water, making sure the water does not touch bottom of bowl. Whisk constantly until fluffy, thick, and hot, 8 to 10 minutes. Add espresso mixture. Remove from heat.

3. Return bowl to mixer, and beat on medium speed until cool, about 10 minutes. Have ready an ice-water bath.

4. Whip cream in a chilled bowl until soft peaks form. Add one-fourth of whipped cream to egg mixture; whisk thoroughly. Fold in remainder of whipped cream. Set mixture in ice-water bath; transfer both to refrigerator.

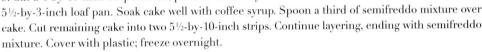

5. Cut a 4-by-10-inch strip of cake; place in a 10½-by-5½-by-3-inch loaf pan. Soak cake well with coffee syrup. Spoon a third of semifreddo mixture over cake. Cut remaining cake into two 5½-by-10-inch strips. Continue layering, ending with semifreddo mixture. Cover with plastic; freeze overnight.

6. When ready to serve, soften in refrigerator, 10 to 20 minutes. Using an ice-cream scoop, form balls, and place on dessert plates. Top with chocolate sauce, and dust with cocoa powder.

chocolate sheet cake | **makes one 10-by-15-inch cake**

 Unsalted butter, for pan
½ cup all-purpose flour, plus
 more for pan
½ cup unsweetened cocoa powder
 Pinch of salt
½ teaspoon baking powder
4 large eggs, separated
1 cup sugar
1 teaspoon pure vanilla extract

1. Heat oven to 350°. Butter a 15¼-by-10¼-by-¾-inch jelly-roll pan. Line with parchment, and butter again. Flour the pan, and set aside.

2. In a large bowl, sift together flour, cocoa powder, salt, and baking powder. Set aside.

3. In the bowl of an electric mixer fitted with the paddle attachment, cream egg yolks and sugar until fluffy. Beat in 3 tablespoons boiling water and the vanilla. Working in three additions, fold the reserved flour mixture into the egg-yolk mixture.

4. Beat egg whites until stiff but not dry. Whisk one-fourth of whites into the batter. Fold in the remaining whites. Transfer batter to prepared pan.

5. Bake until cake springs back when gently pressed, about 15 minutes. Transfer to a wire rack to cool.

coffee syrup | **makes about ½ cup**

½ cup sugar
2 tablespoons Kahlúa liqueur

Combine sugar and ¼ cup water in a small saucepan. Bring liquid to a boil, and stir until sugar has dissolved. Remove pan from heat. Stir in Kahlúa; let cool completely.

warm chocolate sauce | **makes about 1 cup**

6 ounces bittersweet chocolate,
¾ cup plus 1 tablespoon
 heavy cream

Chop chocolate, and place in a small bowl. Pour cream into a small saucepan; scald. Pour cream over chocolate; let stand 5 minutes. Stir until smooth. Set in a hot-water bath until ready to use.

72 *Served right in their waxed-paper wrappers, these ice-cream sandwiches are a casual, old-fashioned summer treat. The vanilla cookies, flavored with ground ginger and minced crystallized ginger, hold homemade peach ice cream. If you don't want to make your own, buy the best-quality ice cream you can find. If peach is not available, try vanilla.*

72 peach ice-cream sandwiches

5 tablespoons unsalted butter,
  room temperature
1 cup sugar
½ teaspoon pure vanilla extract
4 large egg whites,
  room temperature
1 cup sifted all-purpose flour
  Pinch of salt
2 teaspoons ground ginger
1 tablespoon minced crystallized
  ginger (see the Guide)
  Peach Ice Cream (recipe
  follows), softened

These sandwiches are best eaten within two days of being made. Let them soften in the refrigerator for fifteen minutes before serving. | **makes 12 sandwiches**

1. Heat oven to 375°. Cut two 12-by-16-inch rectangles from parchment paper. On each piece of parchment, draw twelve 3½-inch circles with a pencil. Place each piece of parchment, pencil-side down, on a baking sheet.

2. In the bowl of an electric mixer fitted with the paddle attachment, cream butter and sugar on medium-high speed until pale yellow, about 4 minutes. Add the vanilla and egg whites; beat until combined, scraping down the sides of the bowl with a rubber spatula. Add the flour, salt, ground ginger, and crystallized ginger. Beat on low speed until just incorporated.

3. Spoon a heaping tablespoon of batter onto each circle. With back of a spoon, spread evenly to edges.

4. Bake until cookies are golden brown around edges, about 12 minutes; rotate sheets twice during baking for even browning. Transfer sheets to wire racks to cool completely.

5. Spoon about ½ cup of peach ice cream on bottom of a cookie. Top with another one, and press down gently, forcing ice cream to edges. Freeze until firm, then wrap in plastic; return to freezer. Repeat with remaining cookies and ice cream. Freeze sandwiches at least 2 hours before serving.

5 large ripe peaches
  (about 2 pounds)
4 teaspoons freshly squeezed
  lemon juice
1¾ cups sugar
2 tablespoons peach schnapps
2¼ cups milk
2⅔ cups heavy cream
8 large egg yolks
  Pinch of salt
1 teaspoon pure vanilla extract

peach ice cream | **makes 6 cups**

This peach ice cream, spiked with a bit of schnapps, is a satisfying dessert all by itself.

1. Bring a medium saucepan of water to a boil; have ready an ice-water bath. Place peaches in boiling water, and cook 1 to 2 minutes. Using a slotted spoon, transfer peaches to ice-water bath. Peel and pit peaches, reserving skin and pits. Slice each peach into 10 wedges.

2. Place wedges in a nonreactive saucepan; stir in lemon juice and 2 tablespoons sugar. Set over medium-high heat, and cook, stirring occasionally, until the peaches are tender and the liquid has thickened slightly, 10 to 15 minutes. Let cool.

3. Stir peach schnapps into peach mixture. Transfer to a food processor, and process until a chunky purée forms, 10 to 15 pulses. Set the purée aside.

4. Combine milk, cream, peach skins, and peach pits in a medium saucepan. Bring liquid to a boil. Reduce heat to medium low, and simmer 5 minutes. Cover, and let stand 15 minutes.

5. In the bowl of an electric mixer fitted with whisk attachment, combine egg yolks, salt, remaining sugar, and vanilla. Beat at medium-high speed until mixture is thick and pale yellow, about 3 minutes.

6. Strain milk mixture into the egg mixture; discard solids. Beat at low speed to combine.

7. Return new mixture to saucepan; have ready an ice-water bath. Cook over low heat, stirring constantly, until thick enough to coat back of a wooden spoon. Pass mixture through a sieve set over a medium bowl. Place bowl in ice-water bath, and chill.

8. Stir in the peach purée. Freeze in an ice-cream maker according to manufacturer's instructions, working in two batches if necessary. Store ice cream in an airtight container.

73 black-and-white peanut bar

2 pints chocolate ice cream
64 Nabisco's Biscos Sugar
   Wafers, "Creme Filling"
   (about 1 box)
2 pints vanilla ice cream
6 ounces semisweet
   chocolate, chopped
2 teaspoons vegetable shortening
⅓ cup unsalted roasted peanuts,
   roughly chopped

You can make this cake without the formal parchment-paper collar crafted in step seven; just let the melted chocolate drip down the sides of the cake, for a more casual look. | **serves 8**

1. Cut a 5-by-24-inch rectangle out of parchment paper, and set aside. Cut a 4-by-7 ½-inch rectangle out of cardboard or Foamcore.

2. Using a spoon, spread 1 tablespoon chocolate ice cream across the cardboard. Arrange 16 sugar wafers over cardboard (we laid 10 wafers side by side over the lower half of the cardboard; then we made two rows of three wafers, laid end to end, over the top half of the cardboard). You should have a flat, single layer of wafers. This will become the bottom of the cake.

3. Microwave both the chocolate and the vanilla ice cream until softened, about 20 seconds. Transfer the chocolate ice cream to a medium mixing bowl, and transfer the vanilla ice cream to another one. Stir both ice creams with a rubber spatula; place the bowl of vanilla ice cream in the freezer.

4. Using a small offset spatula, spread 2 cups chocolate ice cream as evenly as possible over the wafer layer. Arrange 16 more sugar wafers, as described in step two, on top of the ice cream. Transfer the cake and the bowl of chocolate ice cream to the freezer for 15 minutes.

5. Remove the cake and the bowl of vanilla ice cream from the freezer. Stir the ice cream with a rubber spatula to resoften it, and spread 2 cups vanilla ice cream as evenly as possible over the wafers. Arrange 16 more sugar wafers, as described in step two, on top of the ice cream. Transfer the cake and the bowl of vanilla ice cream to the freezer for 15 minutes more.

6. Repeat the layering process, making one more chocolate and one more vanilla layer, with only one wafer layer in between; chill the cake after making each new layer. End with the layer of vanilla ice cream on the top. Transfer cake to the freezer, and chill cake until completely hard, at least 1 hour.

7. Using a long serrated knife, trim ¼ inch from all sides of the cake, making them even. Wrap the parchment around the sides of the cake, extending ½ inch above top layer; secure the seam with a small dollop of ice cream. Return cake to freezer.

8. Set a heat-proof bowl or the top of a double boiler over a pan of barely simmering water. Place the chocolate and the shortening in the bowl, and stir occasionally until melted, about 7 minutes. Remove the bowl from heat; let chocolate stand until cool but still liquid.

9. Remove cake from freezer, and pour the melted chocolate over the top. Using a spatula, quickly spread chocolate so it meets all four edges of the paper collar. Sprinkle the chopped peanuts over the chocolate. Return cake to freezer, and chill cake until it has completely hardened.

10. When ready to serve, place cake on a serving plate, and peel off the paper collar.

73 *An homage to the Nutty Buddy ice cream cone, this cake is a mélange of melted semisweet chocolate, cream-filled sugar wafers, and vanilla and chocolate ice cream. The top is dotted with chopped peanuts. Like all of our ice-cream cakes, it's not difficult to construct, but it does take some patience to make and chill the layers. The parchment collar is especially fun to peel off at the table.*

The Guide

Items pictured but not listed are from private collections. Addresses and telephone numbers of sources may change prior to or following publication, as may price and availability of any item.

front cover
Martha's shirt *by Comme des Garçons.* **Hair and makeup** *by Sara Johnson with the Sarah Laird Agency.* **Clothes** *styled by Inge Fonteyne with The Agency.* **Green pressed-glass cake stands,** $49 for 8" plate (KJP001), $52 for 10" plate (KJP002), $59 for 12" plate (KJP003), or $149 for set of all three (KJP004), *from Martha By Mail; 800-950-7130 or www.marthabymail.com.*

page 6
Green pressed-glass cake stand *from Martha By Mail, see above.*

Cakes

pages 14 and 15
Special thanks to Lois Milman.

page 18
Nineteenth-century marble bistro table, $1,450, *from Rooms & Gardens, 290 Lafayette Street, New York, NY 10012; 212-431-1297.*

page 19
Hand-blown glass vase, $33, *from L. Becker Flowers, 217 East 83rd Street, New York, NY 10028; 212-439-6001.*

page 21
3"-by-1½" Entreme baking rings, $4.00 each, *from Bridge Kitchenware, 214 East 52nd Street, New York, NY 10022; 212-838-6746.*

page 22
Victorian silver-plate cake knife *from I. Freeman & Son, Inc., 120 East 56th Street, Suite 440, New York, NY 10022; 212-759-6900.*

page 23
Cooling racks, $5.95 to $30, depending on size, *from Bridge Kitchenware, see above.* **Nineteenth-century polished-steel table** *from Rooms & Gardens, see above.*

page 26
Faux bois on tole tray, $195, *from H, 335 East 9th Street, New York, NY 10003; 212-477-2631.*

page 27
Crystallized ginger *available from Royal Pacific Foods, 2700 Garden Road, Suite G, Monterey, CA 93940; 800-551-5284 for nearest retailer.*

page 28
Nineteenth-century polished-steel table *from Rooms & Gardens, see above.*

page 29
Wedgwood White bread-and-butter plates, $12 each, *from Wedgwood; 800-677-7860 for nearest store.*

page 39
Berry brambles and wild rose hips *from Green Valley Growers, 10450 Cherry Ridge Road, Sebastopol, CA 95472; 707-823-5583.* **Italian mascarpone,** $10 per 500-gram tub, *from Dean & DeLuca, 560 Broadway, New York, NY 10012; 212-431-1691 or 800-221-7714.* **7" spiked pillars and 7" and 10" separator plates** *available from New York Cake & Baking Distributor, 56 West 22nd Street, New York, NY 10010; 212-675-2253 or 800-942-2539.*

Spoon Desserts

page 43
9" white ironstone plate, $14, *from Linda Rosen Antiques at the Tomato Factory, 2 Somerset Street, Hopewell, NJ 08525; 609-466-9833.*

page 44
Rialto wineglass, $130, *from Takashimaya, 693 Fifth Avenue, New York, NY 10022; 212-350-0100 or 800-753-2038.*

page 46
Rose-glass salad plate *from Bergdorf Goodman, 754 Fifth Avenue, New York, NY 10019; 212-753-7300.*

page 47
7" Venetian-glass dessert plate, $50, *from Gardner & Barr, 213 East 60th Street, New York, NY 10022; 212-752-0555.*

page 48
4½-cup porcelain terrine mold or 1⅛-quart enameled cast-iron terrine mold *available from Bridge Kitchenware, 214 E. 52nd Street, New York, NY 10022; 212-838-1901/6746 or 800-274-3435.*

page 49
Creamware dinner plate by Wedgwood, $5,250 for set of 12, *from Bardith Ltd., 901 Madison Avenue, New York, NY 10021; 212-737-3775.* **George III-period silver-gilt knife,** $6,250 for a service for 12, *from James Robinson, Inc., 480 Park Avenue, New York, NY 10022; 212-752-6166.*

page 51
Victorian engraved-glass plate, $895 for set of 9 (#S7046), *from James II Galleries, Ltd., 11 East 57th Street, 4th Floor, New York, NY 10022; 212-355-7040.*

page 52
Venetian-glass champagne glasses, part of a 21-piece dessert set, $1,875, *from Malmaison Antiques, 253 East 74th Street, New York, NY 10021; 212-288-7569.* **George II-period sterling-silver spoons,** $5,500 for service of 12, *from James Robinson, Inc., see above.*

page 53
Napoleon III footed serving dish by Sèvres, part of a set, $1,200, *from Malmaison Antiques, see above.* **Sterling-silver reproduction Irish Rib dessert forks,** $175 each, *from James Robinson, Inc., see above.*

page 54
Candied orange zest *available from Dean & DeLuca, 560 Broadway, New York, NY 10021; 212-431-1691 or 800-221-7714.*

page 57
9" white ironstone soup plate, $22, *from Linda Rosen Antiques at the Tomato Factory, see above.*

Pies & Tarts

page 61
Flan rings or fluted tartlet tins *available from New York Cake & Baking Distributor, 56 West 22nd Street, New York, NY 10010; 212-675-2253 or 800-942-2539.*

page 64
Stainless-steel rectangular flan form, $25 for 21" form, $20 for 13" form, *from Bridge Kitchenware, 214 East 52nd Street, New York, NY 10022; 212-838-1901 or 800-274-3435.* **Almond paste** *available from Dean & DeLuca, 560 Broadway, New York, NY 10021; 212-431-1691 or 800-221-7714.*

page 65
Blanched almond flour *available from Dean & DeLuca, see above.*

page 67
Fresh figs *available seasonally from Greenleaf Produce Company, 1955 Jerrold Avenue, San Francisco, CA 94124; 415-647-2991.*

page 70
Bench knife (or dough scraper), $8.95, *from Bridge Kitchenware, see above.*

page 71
Glass compote, $19, *from Linda Rosen Antiques at the Tomato Factory, 2 Somerset Street, Hopewell, NJ 08525; 609-466-9833.*
Linen bedspread from France used as tablecloth, $1,200, *from Takashimaya, 693 Fifth Avenue, New York, NY 10022; 212-350-0100 or 800-753-2038.*

pages 80 and 81
9" 18-gauge aluminum perforated pie tin, $9.99; **9" 16-gauge French pie tin,** $19.99; **and #4 pastry tip,** 99¢, *from New York Cake & Baking Distributor, 56 West 22nd Street, New York, NY 10010; 212-675-2253 or 800-942-2539.*

Fruit Desserts

page 82
Fresh figs *available seasonally from Greenleaf Produce Company, 1955 Jerrold Avenue, San Francisco, CA 94124; 415-647-2991.*

page 89
Wilton #16 star tip, 99¢, *from New York Cake & Baking Distributor, 56 West 22nd Street, New York, NY 10010; 212-675-2253 or 800-942-2539.*

page 92
9" Queen's Ware Traditional Plain salad bowl *from Wedgwood (import only); 800-677-7860 for nearest store.*

page 94
Fresh red currants, $4.95 per pint, *available seasonally from Dean & DeLuca, 560 Broadway, New York, NY 10021; 212-431-1691 or 800-221-7714.*

page 97
Napkin by Archipelago, $27, *from Barneys New York, 660 Madison Avenue, New York, NY 10021; 212-826-8900.*

Cookies

page 103
Valrhona Dutch processed cocoa powder, $8 per pound, *from New York Cake & Baking Distributor, 56 West 22nd Street, New York, NY 10010; 212-675-2253 or 800-942-2539.*
Silpat baking mats, $18 for 11¼"-by-16 ½" mat (KSP002), $27 for 16 ½"-by-24 ¼" mat (KSP001), *from Martha By Mail; 800-950-7130 or www.marthabymail.com.*

page 107
Candied orange peel *available from Dean & DeLuca, 560 Broadway, New York, NY 10021; 212-431-1691 or 800-221-7714.*

page 108
Ateco fluted square cutters, $39.98 for 5-piece set, 1⅛" to 3¼" (#5203), *from New York Cake & Baking Distributor, see above.* **Silpat baking mats** *from Martha By Mail, see above.*

page 113
Silpat baking mats *from Martha By Mail, see above.*

Frozen Desserts

pages 116 and 119
Grapefruit-Campari sorbet, $27.50 for 5 quarts, **and green-apple sorbet,** $34 for 5 quarts, *from Ciao Bella Gelato Company, 262 Mott Street, New York, NY 10012; 800-343-5286 or www.ciaobellagelato.com.*

page 120
Circa-1930 French glazed-ceramic café-au-lait bowls, $35 each, *from Lucullus, 610 Chartres Street, New Orleans, LA 70130; 504-528-9620.*

page 121
Starbucks Dark Roast Espresso Swirl ice cream *available in supermarkets nationwide.*

page 124
Cream of coconut, $4.50 for 16 ounces,

from Dean & DeLuca, 560 Broadway, New York, NY 10021; 212-431-1691 or 800-221-7714.

page 129
Silpat baking mats, $18 for 11¼"-by-16 ½" mat (KSP002), $27 for 16 ½"-by-24 ¼" mat (KSP001), *from Martha By Mail; 800-950-7130 or www.marthabymail.com.* **Coconut sorbet,** $24.95 for four pints, *available from Ciao Bella Gelato Company, see above.*

page 135
Crystallized ginger *available from Royal Pacific Foods, 2700 Garden Road, Suite G, Monterey, CA 93940; 800-551-5284 for nearest retailer.*

If you have enjoyed this book, please join us as a subscriber to MARTHA STEWART LIVING *magazine. The annual subscription rate is $26 for ten issues. Call toll-free 800-999-6515, or visit our web site, www.marthastewart.com.*

Other books available in The Best of Martha Stewart Living series:

DECORATING FOR THE HOLIDAYS (CHRISTMAS WITH MARTHA STEWART LIVING, VOLUME 2)

DECORATING DETAILS

GREAT PARTIES

CHRISTMAS WITH MARTHA STEWART LIVING (VOLUME 1)

GOOD THINGS

GREAT AMERICAN WREATHS

HOW TO DECORATE

HANDMADE CHRISTMAS

WHAT TO HAVE FOR DINNER

SPECIAL OCCASIONS

HOLIDAYS

Photography Credits

William Abranowicz
front cover, pages 6, 18, 22, 23, 28, 29, 32, 33

Anthony Amos
page 9

Christopher Baker
pages 3, 30, 34, 35, 65, 70–72, 91, 95, 134

Anita Calero
page 39

Carlton Davis
pages 37, 111

Todd Eberle
page 92

Dana Gallagher
pages 40, 86, 100, 103–105, 107, 109, 110, 113, back cover (second from top)

Gentl & Hyers
pages 8, 93, 115

Thibault Jeanson
page 64

Michael Mundy
page 133

Victoria Pearson
pages 19, 44, 46, 47, 55, 99, 112, back cover (top)

Maria Robledo
pages 2, 4, 5, 10, 14, 15, 17, 25, 26, 43, 49, 51–53, 57, 58, 66, 67, 69, 74–77, 81, 82, 87, 94, 97, 116, 120, 122, 123, 127, 129–131, 137, 138, back cover (third from top, bottom)

Victor Schrager
page 63

Index